OUR CORN

BUDE

BOSCASTLE

PORT ISAAC

PADSTOW
St. MINVER
ROCK

BODMIN

LANHYDROCK

BUGLE

St. AUSTELL

MEVAGISSEY

TRURO

REDRUTH

CAMBORNE

St. IVES

FALMOUTH

PENZANCE
SENNEN
LANDS END
HELSTON

TREEN

COVERACK

OUR CORNWALL

The Stories of Cornish Men and Women

Recorded by

Jack Gillespie

TABB HOUSE

First published in Great Britain, 1988
Tabb House, 7 Church Street, Padstow, Cornwall PL28 8BG

ISBN 0 907018 62 9

All royalties from this book go to the John Betjeman Centre for the
Elderly, Wadebridge, Cornwall

Typeset by St. George Printing Works Ltd., Redruth, Cornwall
Printed in Great Britain by A. Wheaton & Co. Ltd, Exeter

For my brother Tom Gillespie, a member of the Cornish Association of New South Wales, Australia.

PREFACE

I had an uncle by marriage who died aged ninety-six. He told me tales which spanned the Victorian era; for example, how his grandmother refreshed with cups of tea soldiers returning from the Crimean war. Because I was foolish enough not to record his memoirs, many have vanished in the slipstream of death.

When I visited Lanhydrock House near Bodmin, its evocation of life in times gone by reminded me of my uncle's reminiscences and awoke in me a keen desire to hear the stories of those who had lived and worked there. I was fortunately able to track down and talk to a number of people, some of whose tales are included in this book and more of whose are now on tapes, lodged with the National Trust at Lanhydrock. Talking to those Lanhydrock folk led on to conversations with men and women representing a wide variety of occupations and different generations throughout Cornwall.

The people in this book are by definition ordinary folk who have lived and worked in Cornwall, some to a ripe old age. Not to repeat my previous error and because since my uncle's day I have spent twenty years wedded to a tape recorder as a radio and television producer I have chosen to let the words and actions of these people speak for themselves.

I believe the quality of their lives provides a refreshing perspective on the concept of ordinariness. Because they are the stuff of Cornish heritage, with tales told and problems bravely faced, this is truly THEIR book.

Jack Gillespie

CONTENTS

Page

LIST OF ILLUSTRATIONS

35. Horses and waggons owned by Jack's relations. These took clay to port and on return from Par to Bugle the horses would get a drink of beer at The Norway Inn
36. Ships like these exported clay from Par early in the 20th century
37. Stan Yelland, with a clay shovel
38. William Chellew, a farrier in the First World War
39. The last blacksmith at St Minver
40. William, extreme right, with the tenor bell of St Endellion Church
41. The further part of the white building was the Chellew's home
42. Mr John Smith outside William's old smithy, which he saved from demolition
43. Competitors in a milking competition in the early 1900s
44. Jack Boney
45. Jack at Copplestone Farm
46. Harry Champion, 2nd World War Light Infantryman
47. Green keeper at St Enodoc Golf Club
48. John and Mary May with their 9 children
49. The gatehouse at Lanhydrock, where the May children went to Sunday school
50. The Hon. Misses Everilda and Violet Robartes attending children at a village tea party
51. Esme Dawe, Mayor of Bodmin in a mayorial procession
52. Richard and Esme Dawe, mayors of Bodmin
53. Owie Jewell, Honoured Burgess of Bodmin
54. John Corin, bank manager
55. Mr Corin at the ruins of his ancestor the smuggler John Corlyon's cottage
56. John studying a painting of the Battle of Algiers, 1816, in which Corlyon took part
57. Dr Frank Harvey and his two daughters
58. The Padstow ferry used by passengers to Rock including John Betjeman and Dr Harvey
59. Robert Rowe at St Lawrence's Hospital
60. Amy Beswetherick, district nurse
61. Amy at the age of 92
62. Lily May being interviewed by the author with BBC film unit at her old Lanhydrock school, where Elizabeth McGuigan taught

The photographs of Walter Boyd were taken by Christopher Nicholson and that of the Padstow ferry by Ray Bishop. Permission to reproduce them is gratefully acknowledged.

The names under the photographs of Billy Johns and Tom Dyer opposite p.110 should be transposed.

Photograph no.14 does not show the former post office at St. Minver; caption no.41 correctly identifies it as the Chellews' old home.

DICK PAUL

Cornish Coastguard

Dick Paul, stocky, bronzed and tough, lives in Penzance. In an action-packed life which he describes as ordinary, he has been a fisherman, a leading-seaman gunner in the Navy and a coastguard. More important to Dick Paul than the medals he has been awarded during his active life, is the knowledge of difficult commitments well and truly done. This is his story.

I was a fisherman before the war and I didn't know a lot about morse or semaphore, but after I joined the Coastguards we got training every month from the district officer on the station. After nine months we went down to St Ives and qualified by examination in every subject on the course – navigation, chart work, life-saving, coast rescue, morse, semaphore, splices, hitches, that sort of thing. If anybody failed a subject he could try again after six months. Fortunately I didn't need to.

During the war the Admiralty took over the Hull trawler, *Capstan*, and I served on her. I remember vividly one night an event that took place here, almost on our doorstep. It was in 1942 and the *Capstan* was in Mount's Bay. The Germans were bombing Penzance. We saw an enemy plane come out of Penzance and fly across the bay. We thought it was going in to bomb Newlyn. It was bright moonlight, which lit up the concrete roads of a coastal estate. The guns of the *Capstan* were aimed and fired. If we had missed him he would have known exactly where we were. Luckily we got him first shot – we laid the gunfire just ahead of him so that he flew into it. The *Capstan* did other good work during the war. We crossed over many times in the rescue at Dunkirk, and later were on convoy duties.

Recently I had an extraordinary follow-up to the incident in Mount's Bay. I met a fellow from Hull in a bus queue in Penzance. We got talking and it transpired that he had come on

1

holiday to try and trace anybody who had been on the trawler *Capstan* during the war. He told me he had been there a week trying to find anyone who had been on the ship with his father. I said there were only a couple of us left now. He turned out to be the son of the skipper of the *Capstan*. So we got together and I told him all I knew about the ship. He said meeting me had made his holiday.

In January, 1946, I came out of the Navy and joined the Coastguard Service. I was in it until I retired in 1974. I was in the same station, Treen, all that time. Treen is near Porthcurno the cable and wireless station, coming south round from Land's End. We had our lookout near the Logan Rock headland. It was a very busy station in my day. We did an awful lot of cliff rescues. We also had bad weather watch stations and you went on these when the wind force was over four. So there was the constant watch station and the occasional lookout. When the constant watch station thought the wind force was over four, and the visibility under the mile, they'd put the bad weather watch on. We had a lot of trouble in those days before they brought in the Decca navigational system for ships. Ships would run in on shore. We'd fire a flashing sound to warn them off and we had the international sound signal, two shorts and a long, to tell them 'You're standing into danger'. We only had eleven wrecks in the area all the time I was there.

You were on the telephone all the time. In the summer you'd probably have to come out three or four times a week to rescue people cut off by the tide, fallen down a cliff or adrift in dinghies and all that sort of thing. I've been in over a hundred rescues of this sort.

There was a coastal liaison at St Just. In those days they'd liaise with Land's End radio; Land's End radio would pick up an SOS or Mayday, push it into the coastguard liaison station. It, in turn, would inform the coastguard station concerned, which would activate the life-saving team that would consist of ten or a dozen men and also the lifeboat. So we not only became the action station but also the lifeboat launching station. When the ball was in our court we did what we were supposed to do, then we would inform the coastguard liaison station and it would tell Land's End radio. They, in turn, would tell the ship, so the message was passed on from channel to channel and

2

everybody was in the picture.

The life-rescue team were men who were trained to bring men ashore, to use breeches buoys, to make contact, to fire rockets and so on. They had about six exercises a year. A team was attached to every coastguard station. If you had a two-pounder rocket, you'd have eight men; if you had a six-pounder, you'd have ten men. If you had a rescue rocket – a helluva thing that was jet-propelled – you'd have twenty men. They were all kinds; carpenters, masons, farm workers, fishermen. You'd fire a maroon to alert them and they'd come running. The coast rescue teams came under the Coastguard Service. They were the Coast Life Saving Corps, grand men. They were expert at getting men ashore by breeches buoy.

A coastguard could never order a lifeboat to sea. You could only advise the lifeboat secretary. You might say, 'We advise launch,' but it was up to him entirely. Once the lifeboat was launched, the coxswain would come on radio at once to the coastguard. When he was at sea, he got in touch with Land's End radio. In my earlier years there wasn't a lot of radio. It was only in the latter years they introduced walkie-talkies. In those earlier days, we might be called out from the station and have to walk for miles along the coast to find a ship and then run back to a farm with a phone which might be half a mile or two miles away. We had to get to a telephone when we were searching along the coast and this normally happened in the middle of the night. Local people knew where the telephones were. Nowadays with walkie-talkies there's not that problem between searchers and the station.

I remember an old coaster, the *Hemsley I*, that was going over from Liverpool to Brest on a one-way passage to be broken up. She ran ashore in the fog, and the Captain reported she was in the Land's End area. We walked from Treen to Lamorna Cove, about four miles, searching every nook and cranny and couldn't find anything at all. We reported and they said, 'You must have missed it, Mr Paul, you'd better go back.' Then, another message came in. Men had been spotted sitting on a rock just above high water. Back we went but found nothing. When we got back to the station I reported, 'That ship is not here, repeat, not here.' Back came a message that the ship had now been found – near Padstow miles away, on the north coast, a wreck. This shows how much walking and searching there was in days gone by. It also shows, if a careful watch is not maintained and charts looked at often, how wrong captains can be in assuming where they are.

These coastal paths could be dangerous.

This coast was known as the graveyard of shipping. It was where the Penlee lifeboat went down. The lifeboat was launched in a force 12 wind with seas sixty feet high. It went to the rescue of the *Union Star,* which had eight people on board including a woman and two girls, and was drifting fast towards high cliffs in the marine trap of Mount's Bay. Driving rain made conditions worse, and the wind made it impossible for the helicopter involved in the rescue attempt to hover over the boat. The lifeboat took four people off and while doing so was twice washed onto the deck of the *Union Star* before sliding back into the sea. The last radio message from the lifeboat said they were making another attempt to get off the rest of the people. Then there was silence. Later, the *Union Star* was found lying on her side and the water was littered with floating pieces of the *Solomon Brown.* I knew the crew of the *Solomon Brown* well, and the coxswain who used to come here to see me.

A small French oil tanker, the *San Guenol,* was one ship that got into trouble. There had been a heavy swell and a bit of storm and low visibility. The fellow on lookout gave me a shout, 'There's something gone in around the corner. She's gone out of my sight.' Halfway down the cove I could hear shouting. I went down while the lad was standing by up at the station. When I got down, I saw a man in the sea washing in and out, up and down, on the slip. There was a hell of a sea. I suppose I was a fool, but I went in and grabbed him. I managed to pull him up on the shore and carried him to a cottage owned by a chap we called Captain Jack. We got him round. He was a Frenchman and he didn't understand us. I said to Jack, 'Give me a paper and pencil. There's a ship here somewhere.' I drew the coastline and showed it to the fellow and he pinpointed the place exactly. I fired a rocket and the boys came down and we searched the place. We thought we saw somebody down below us flashing a torch. I got out the ropes and prepared to go down to see if there was anybody down there. I went down hand over hand and got aboard the wreck, hanging on to the lifeline.

There was a big forty-gallon oil drum butting up against the cliff bottom and causing sparks. In the dark it was shining like a torch. But there was no one there. It turned out there were no other survivors. There had been eleven of the crew drowned. That chap was the only survivor.

Twelve months later, a Catholic priest came to see us. He'd come over for the opening of Coventry Cathedral. The survivor of that wreck had been his brother. He told us that it was the third time his brother had been wrecked. He was now an onion farmer. The priest asked 'Are you Dick Paul?' and when I said I was he asked me to take him down to the scene where his brother was saved. I told him it was a long way down and steep. He said he didn't mind, so we went down and he blessed the water. It was a kind of religious ceremony. When we came back to the station for coffee, I said, 'Sorry, but I haven't got anything stronger.'

'Don't worry,' he answered, 'I've got a little bottle in my case!' So we had coffee and brandy. He was a nice fellow.

I expect the Imperial Service Medal I received was mainly in recognition of the rescue of many men from some of the most famous post-war shipwrecks around Land's End. I assisted in rescue work at the wrecks of the *Juan Ferrer*, the *Vert Prairial* and the St Ives lugger, the *Nazarenc*. I think the most memorable incident was when we brought eighteen people out of a cave cut off by the tide at Green Bay near Porthcurno. I took a blind boy on my shoulders 200 feet up the cliff.

There was another wreck described in my album, which I call *A Great Mystery*. The weather was good, the visibility was good, yet the wreck happened. It began when I got a report of a heavy smell of diesel oil and to me that could only mean that something had run ashore. I sent a fellow back to find out if there was a wreck. He phoned to tell me 'Porthchapel is full of bodies.' I asked where the ship was. 'Ashore on Wireless Point' he said.

When we got down there, we picked up seventeen bodies, all drowned barring one man, who was the mate. Only a couple of years ago I learned the truth about this tragedy. I discovered they had all been drinking. You would hardly believe it but I've seen vessels come up around Land's End with nobody at all on the bridge. The watchman has maybe gone aft to make a cup of tea. This used to happen often and we had to report each case. We would send a warning rocket over the vessel and I've seen a fellow hurry out to take the wheel. Remember Land's End can be very dangerous. It's where southern, eastern and western bound traffic converges. The people in charge are not properly trained and under the Panamanian flag anything can happen. It can be frightening at times. That's why you have to be on your toes.

The timing of calling out a lifeboat is crucial especially in one of the worst areas of the Cornish coast. There are a lot of decisions to be made and if you make a mistake, that's it. The decision whether to advise launching the lifeboat or not is yours. Nowadays they have all mod. cons; all the technology. But in my day we depended more on visual lookouts. When you saw a red flare go up you went into action. There was always good liaison between coastguards and coxswains of lifeboats and also the pilots of helicopters. But the helicopters came in my later years; before them you did it all on shanks' pony.

When we had a call for a missing boat we centralised the gear in one spot and the coast rescue team would fan out from that point, each one with a flash and sound rocket, which could go up a couple of hundred feet and burst. That's how we handled the situation at a distance from the station.

The coastguard headquarters at Falmouth are now the centre of all operations. With radio and radar they can control hundreds and hundreds of miles. So most of the lookouts of my day have gone, and in this respect the coastguards have been cut almost to nothing.

The authorities are taking a calculated risk in closing down the stations. With radio and radar it may not think the stations necessary but what about possible loss of lives through closing them down? There is no man born entitled to take a calculated risk on another man's life. If you were a conscientious watchman – the coastguard has naval training and in my case the experience of a fisherman as well – a star would never drop out of the heavens without him seeing it and the bloke in the next station would say, 'Did you see that star?' 'Yes, I've just logged it.' If you saw something unusual, that shouldn't be, you'd get through to the next station: 'How about this fellow then? He's on a poor course, isn't he? Would you give him a flash?' We'd get out the Aldis lamp and give him a flash. Very little was missed between the men in constant stations and the occasional stations. We lost something worthwhile when we lost those stations. The next station to us was Mousehole, that was six miles away. The one behind us was Tolpidden, that's just around at the first point on Land's End. In fact that was the original Land's End coastal station before they moved it towards the hotel. That was round the corner, so the lookout saw from where he was west towards St Just, but he couldn't see from there round to Lamorna.

With those stations everything could be covered visually. If we saw a vessel coming too near, we'd give him an Aldis warning or two shorts and a long on sound, the international signal for 'You're standing into danger' – and the skipper could alter course. If he was still drawing too near to the shore, you'd fire a big maroon. In the stations you were on the spot and could act immediately.

The way things are now, there is always the chance a ship will fire a flare and no one will see it. I don't think it's a good thing. You saw what happened recently with a pop star's yacht, *Drum*. Luckily there was a retired lieutenant-commander down at Portscatho who happened to see that they were in trouble. There's no coastguard there.

He observed the boat from his lounge window and rang Falmouth who alerted the Falmouth lifeboat and the helicopter at Culdrose. Helicopters can do work that lifeboats never can. On this occasion the helicopter crew took a couple of frogmen with them because when it was reported that the boat had capsized Falmouth coastguard realised there might be people trapped under water, and so it turned out.

The pop-star, Simon le-Bon of the group Duran Duran, was on board with his crew. They were trapped in the capsized boat and their only hope of being rescued was the frogmen. In that situation the lifeboat could not have helped.

Helicopters have caused a revolution in the rescue business. They will never take the place of lifeboats but there's good liaison between them. Lifeboats can go in under cliffs where helicopters cannot, but lifeboats don't carry deep sea divers.

I've been trained to be lowered from a helicopter on rescue

missions. I remember on one particular occasion there was a fellow who swam out to a couple of rocks in front of the look-out station. He had left his glasses on the beach and was nearly blind – he wasn't able to get back. A helicopter was scrambled which flew down and picked me up, then we flew out to the rock and they lowered me down and I got the chap up.

We worked closely with the helicopter pilots, but if there was a dead calm under a cliff they often preferred us to do the rescue from shore because if they came in too close in hot weather when the air was still it could be difficult. They preferred to come in against a breeze. I remember one tough cliff rescue. The Marine Commandos, who were stationed in Devonport, were training along the cliffs. One of them slipped and fell down the cliff. When they come out for cliff climbing training they usually bring their own doctor with them, but this time they were on a running exercise, so they didn't have a medical officer. I went down the cliff on a rope and reached the man. I have never seen anyone so badly injured. He was too smashed up for us to attempt to get him up the cliffs, so a helicopter was called out. I've never seen another rescue like it. It was terrific to stand on that rock ledge with the injured man and watch the helicopter come down alongside me. I had a job to remain standing with the helicopter hovering no more than fifteen feet above me. They had brought a doctor who gave the injured man jabs to put him out. We strapped him up and got him onto the stretcher which was winched to safety.

I rang the colonel the next day to see how the man was. He told me he was coming along all right, and thanked us for our help. I told him it was the helicopter pilot he had to thank.

I can't speak highly enough of the helicopter pilots. The rescue service was developed at Culdrose. In the summer time they do hundreds of sorties and save hundreds of lives. To start with, helicopters were kept there because Culdrose was an air training station and they were there in case an aircraft ditched. As time went on they offered to help us any time we needed them and it snowballed from there. It's a marvellous service.

In my day, I lived coastguard, I slept coastguard and I taught coastguard. I used to say to the men, 'While you're on lookout, don't bat an eyelid. If you're in any doubt, tell me.' Officially they only had to drill four times a year, but I took them once a month. We trained at Treen and I used to tell the lads, 'If anything comes ashore, we've got to pull these people out.' They were all volunteers drawn from all walks of life. I could trust them with anything. When the inspector came out he'd tell me which drilling method he wanted to see. There were A, B, and C, different methods of rescue. But I told him there was no need for me to drill them. 'You tell them which method you want, and they'll do it. They know exactly what to do.' He watched them in action; farm labourers, fishermen, carpenters, masons; and was amazed at how good they were.

I retired from the station in 1974. But I'm still on the go. I do shopping for old people and help them with their gardens. I go up to Newlyn and teach them navigation; I teach them in their houses, fellows that want to go up for their mate's ticket or their skipper's ticket. Two years ago I taught five of them and I'm glad to say all five passed. This winter I expect there will be people who will want to be taught things like knots and splicing; there are so many people here connected with boats and the sea.

TREVOR ENGLAND

Coxswain

Trevor England is coxswain of the Padstow lifeboat and skipper of the fishing boat *Diligence*.

You might say I was destined for the lifeboat service. My family has been connected with it since 1883. My grandfather's brother was in it and my grandfather joined in 1894. He was bowman of his boat. My father joined in 1934 as a second mechanic and I followed in 1958. This continuity, I suppose, gives a historical view of the changes in the service over the last hundred years.

In the nineteenth century Padstow had three lifeboats. There had always been one which was originally a rowing boat. Most of the ships that got involved in difficulties were sailing boats that had come into the river entrance. The lifeboat only had to row out to get the ship that had run ashore or was stuck on the Doom Bar. Then the RNLI started to help ships when they got into difficulties further out at sea. For that they needed lifeboats with power so they brought in the steam lifeboats but these were not a good design and were unsatisfactory. The engineers were battened down below and when boats capsized there was loss of life.

One of the steamboats was the *James Stevenson*, which was lost in 1900. They then brought in a tug. I don't think there was anything else like it in the British Isles. She was over 110 feet and was called the *Helen Peel*. This tug was used to tow a surf lifeboat, the *Edmund Harvey*, which was rigged with oars and sail. When they had to travel a long distance to reach a vessel in trouble it would be too far for the lifeboat crew to row unless the wind was in the right direction, so they used the tug to tow them out close to the casualty and then cast them adrift. They would then complete the rescue and return to the tug. So that's why there were three lifeboats. When the *Helen Peel* left Padstow in 1929 she was replaced by the *Princess Mary* lifeboat, a twin-funnelled petrol-driven boat some sixty-six feet long. The *Edmund Harvey* soon followed the *Helen Peel* as there was no need for her then, but until quite recently she was still going strong as a yacht.

The north Cornish coast is dangerous, and it has hardly any harbours coming down from Bristol. There was coastal trade from Appledore and Bideford, and between there and Hayle there is no other real harbour but Padstow. A little shipping went in and out of Newquay harbour which had a road and railway going down to the quayside, but the next big harbour was Hayle and beyond that Penzance.

When the coastal trade was in its heyday a ship of fifty or seventy-five tons burden was considered a biggish boat. All along the coast the small ports would have had four or five boats calling in each week with grain, potatoes, flour, china clay and so on. The ships were under sail, and if the weather was rough they would easily get blown into the estuary.

Padstow was a port of great importance. There were six yards here building schooners, and the Padstow lifeboat was kept busy going to the aid of vessels that came to grief on the Doom Bar. A local story about the Doom Bar is that a sailor shot a mermaid there and she put a curse on all sailors – but the ridge of sand has always been there. It's been recorded that as far back as the time of Henry VIII sand was being taken by barge from the estuary.

Emigrant ships sailed out of Padstow for Canada. The fare was thirty shillings. I remember one old man who had paid his thirty shillings and gone there. He told me 'We couldn't stick it out there. The Scots could stick it – they were used to the bloody cold. Canada was too cold for us so we came home again.'

The outstanding feature that has changed is the power of the modern RNLI craft. Another big change is in the type of work we do. I don't imagine one call in twelve months would have been made for what were regarded as trivial mishaps. All the calls in the old days were for commercial traders forced into dangerous situations. A bather in trouble would have been unheard of as a reason for call out in my young days. Nowadays we go out for almost anything at all.

One example was a drowning tragedy. Three young lads came down here for a wedding. They were staying at Constantine. On the Friday night they went for a swim and got into trouble. One was pulled out, but the other two were lost. All this happened within fifteen minutes of their arriving at their hotel. We were called out, but there wasn't much hope by the time we got round there. It was a case of flying a flag and patrolling off the beach just in case we saw anything.

What people don't realise is that any callout could end in tragedy for the lifeboat crew. The men on call must muster without delay and the lifeboat is put to sea in the shortest possible time. Everything is done at high speed.

When there is an alarm the coastguard usually gets the first information. He phones the honorary secretary of the lifeboat at Padstow and he in turn phones the shore signalman who fires two maroons from the concrete compound on the quay. The explosion sends a rocket into the sky. As it opens there's a crack and a loud explosion. It has a green star in it and a sound signal which is the same for lifeboat call outs throughout the British Isles. One maroon is for a cliff rescue which is for the Coastguard Service. When we had more than one lifeboat it was two maroons for the small inshore boat and four for the large boat. The maroons have been replaced at some stations by bleepers that are only heard by the lifeboat crewmen who wear them. I think the maroons should be kept. There was an instance at the Scillies when two women and their children were in the sea as the result of an accident, in fog. One of them was treading water, supporting her child, when she heard the maroon and told him "It won't be long before we are rescued now". Hearing it gave her fresh heart and I think it saved her life.

When you're a seaman you get the feel of the job. If you're taking the wheel of a lifeboat in huge seas you actually feel the boat into a situation. It isn't just a case of catching the wheel and that's the boat and this is you. You get bonded together as one – if you don't I doubt if you could do the job.

One night we were called out on a false alarm although it was a genuine mistake. A commercial traveller reported that he had seen a red flare when he was driving from Newquay to Padstow. A couple of years ago I was on the same road and I saw exactly what he must have seen. As you come down the hill, and with a particular sort of sky, the beam of Trevose lighthouse, which is a red flashing light, catches a bright cloud as it revolves. On a clear night that light will loom around and the loom will reflect into the sky. If you weren't expecting it you might well think. 'My God, a red flash,' and assume it was a flare.

It had been blowing west to sou'west and north here for nine or ten days, when the traveller reported what he'd seen. There was one hell of a sea and we launched an hour from low water. When we went round Trevose it was just a mass of white water in front of us. We went over two seas, but the third stove in our wheelhouse windows. Some fifty tons of water poured into the wheelhouse. Tony Warnock called out that he couldn't see – we thought he had lost his sight, but what had happened was that he had been badly cut by the flying glass and the blood had got into his eyes. We all had cuts – I had to have three stitches in my face and the other lads had stitches too. One bloke had three ribs broken. Just after the sea had done all that damage there was an eerie silence which gave us enough time to collect out thoughts. We turned the boat and headed back to the boathouse. Another sea came on behind us and if it hadn't been for that pause – if we'd had another sea break aboard – I don't really know what would have happened. The boat was no longer watertight; we could not have relied on her, and there were men in exposed positions who could easily have been washed overboard.

That was on the *James and Catherine McFarlane* and as a result it was discovered that there was a design fault in the boat that had caused the problem. There was quite an overhang on the deck where the bulkhead went up in the engine room. We had about four feet of overhang with no stanchion underneath. The window came up to the main cabin roof and as the sea fell on it, it depressed the deck and we couldn't open the engine room door. The bar holding the centre of the window parted, and the window blew out and smashed. All of us could have been completely blinded and the next sea could have turned the boat over. We were lucky.

Good came of it, for after our experience all the boats of that type in the fleet had a strengthening bar put in. Another

13

important thing was that the doors had been designed to stop anything outside from coming in. The designers hadn't considered the possibility of the doors needing protection from internal pressure. But once it had come in, the water had to get out somehow. In our case the fifty ton pressure of water that had come in through the broken window blew the doors off their rollers. So following our experience they cut a nine inch flap on the bottom of the doors with press studs in, so that if there was any way water could get in, it would blow the flaps open and run out under the self-draining cockpit. So that was a lesson in design that resulted from a false alarm.

There was another time when the weather was even worse. This was no false alarm. It was when we went to rescue the crew of a Greek ship that went ashore at Port Quin. She had been sheltering in St Ives Bay. The wind had gone to hurricane force gusting at 127 miles an hour. It was nor'west, blowing right into St Ives. It caused devastation in Cornwall; trees were blown down and roofs blown off. The skipper had been asked by the coastguard to take his boat out of St Ives Bay because there was no shelter there and if anything had happened to her anchor she'd have been driven ashore and that would have been the end of her. Why the skipper decided to come this way instead of going round Land's End point I don't know, for if he'd gone round into Mount's Bay he'd have got a lot of shelter there. Anyway he did come this way.

I had gone down to the boathouse in the morning to see if the gale had caused any structural damage to the building. I rang the coastguard about a quarter past eight to see if there was anything moving at all, expecting him to say there were a lot of ships in trouble in the south-west approaches. 'No,' he said, 'But I've just picked up a Mayday relay three miles north of Trevose.' You could practically have spat from the telephone to three miles north of Trevose, it was so close.

When I had looked at the sea that morning I had never expected anything to be there, much less that we would be asked to launch. However, we launched just after nine. In my report afterwards I wrote that I had felt like an insect in a ploughed field. There were just great furrows and furrows of sea. I don't remember seeing any land at all from when we left the boathouse till we arrived at the boat in trouble. The

14

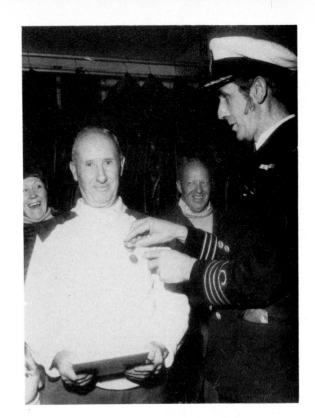

1 Dick Paul receiving the
   Imperial Service Medal

2 Dick's lookout post at Treen

3 Trevor England, Coxswain of the Padstow lifeboat

4 Padstow lifeboat bringing in a boat with a fouled propeller

5   Bill Elvin, South Cornish fisherman

6   Bill's Cornish lugger, the *Erin*

7 Tommy Morrissey, North Cornish fisherman

8 Tommy fishing off Padstow

concentration was such that every sea that came at us was a potential capsize sea. It was enormous – imagine, if you can, a wall of water forty feet high coming at you, that's what each wave was. It's awe-inspiring when you find yourself in an ocean like that where the seas are so phenomenal and yet the boat is coping with it.

People often ask if we are afraid when we go out in seas like that, and I tell them we don't really have time to feel scared because we have to concentrate so much. What it's like for the crew I'm not so sure because they have nothing to do until the rescue starts. For them there is more time to be terrified, but the coxswain has to think what to do. He's at the wheel. On that occasion the seas were terrible and we couldn't do anything. The ship we hoped to rescue went on the rocks and broke in two.

Another tragic event we were involved in was when we lost a ship about eight years ago. Its fore and aft stoved in. Two people were picked up off a life raft twelve hours later, but the skipper was gone with his wife and children. That was a Danish ship, the *Lady Camilla*, loaded with china clay. She'd come out of Par and was going to Liverpool. The tragedy took place the day before Christmas Eve.

The north-west is our prevailing wind. This is the one that causes most problems, when you get a heavy build-up right across the Atlantic. There's always a temptation for a ship to keep going, even in dangerous conditions, because a delay always means a loss of money. It's about eighty miles from Lundy Island to Land's End point, so if they're holed up at Lundy and they know they've got to come around to reach their destination, when there's a lull in the wind they are tempted to leave the shelter and make a run for it. But often by the time they get down here the wind has got up again, and then there's nowhere else to shelter until they get around the point at Land's End.

As a lifeboatman we get called out to different kinds of rescues in very different circumstances and weather. Take any two years, say 1979 and 1980, with the lifeboat *James and Catherine Macfarlane*, which was involved in many rescues. She saved the fishing boat *Girl Anne* at Padstow. She gave help to the cabin cruiser *Gay Dawn* of London when she was in difficulty.

15

When a man was injured aboard the yacht *Tamson II* the lifeboat took the doctor out and escorted the yacht back to the harbour. The yacht *Tarantula* was saved with one man on board, also the catamaran *Palukina* with one man, and the yacht *Peggy*, with nine on board, was safely landed. In 1980 the *James and Catherine Macfarlane* saved the *Bristol Spray* of Avon, recovered the wreckage of the fishing vessel *Camelot Challenger* and gave help to the *Lamorna*. She saved the yacht *Starfish* of Swansea with one man, and escorted the fishing vessel *St Agnes* when its crew of three were in danger. Those are just a few incidents in the life of one lifeboat. They happen all the time.

The choice of a lifeboat coxswain depends on the situation at any given time. We can now call on a crew of twenty-two, and if I suddenly packed up tomorrow, I think without fear or favour, the second coxswain would not want to take over from me. He's a first class man, but he has a lot on his hands. He runs a big farm which takes a lot of his time. Being a coxswain means you have to be always available to do the job properly. We've also had a deputy coxswain who was a dentist, and you can see how difficult it would be for him to take the job. In a situation like this another member of the crew might come in as coxswain, maybe someone who has a lifelong connection with the sea. You might have a second coxswain who is a good yachtsman and very good and very handy in a boat. He's a great asset as a member of the crew, but he's not a fulltime seaman in the deepest sense. If no one in the boat wanted the job then the Institute would advertise, as they do now, around the coast. We have to have a medical every five years until we are fifty-five and then every year after that.

Our latest lifeboat, with myself as coxswain, was commissioned in Padstow in April 1985. This is the *James Burrough*, named after the grandfather of the donor, Miss H. B. Allen. The completely new hull design of this Tyne class lifeboat has made possible a speed of eighteen knots. Its active radius is 120 miles and it brings new safety factors into our rescue work around these treacherous coasts. There's seating capacity for seven men, and this is very important because in very bad weather the men must be seated and strapped in. The old pulling and sailing lifeboats carried about thirteen or fourteen men. There were twelve oars, six aside and one coxswain and possibly a bowman or lookout.

I think the lifeboat crews and coxswains are the greatest club in the world. I've travelled around with staff coxswain Tom Beattie who came from Orkney. He lives in Arbroath now. He delivers boats that are on refit or replacement boats. I know the coxswains at Oban and Holyhead, and the men at Fishguard, Mumbles, and Tenby. We meet when we take boats in or we can ring each other up. Padstow is a stopping off place for boats on passage. If a boat is coming down the coast, Padstow is a good stop before Land's End and Plymouth. There are about half a dozen yards in the British Isles that specifically do lifeboat refits. There are about 130 offshore lifeboats.

The night we came back after the disaster to the Greek ship, Mat Lethbridge the coxswain over at the Scillies rang my wife to know if we were back. He was so concerned. Similarly last year when I was listening to the radio and heard Mat Lethbridge talking to the coastguard about a yacht he had picked up thirty miles west of Trevose I rang Mat's wife Pat, and told her what was happening and how long he would be. There's a good spirit in the service.

This story might give you an idea of what lifeboat service is like.

BILL ELVIN AND TOMMY MORRISSEY

Fishermen

BILL ELVIN

For the last eighty-five years Bill Elvin has lived in Mevagissey, now grown from a fishing village to a modern tourist centre. Bill's grandfather and father were fishermen; you could say the sea was in their blood. Bill's knowledge of this part of the Cornish coast is hard to rival.

I was fishing even before I left school at fourteen. In those early days we would go out with another seine boat for mackerel – two boats; a big one and a small one. This was in the August holidays when I was thirteen and still at school. We'd be fishing off the beach at Pentewan, where the caravans are now. The mackerel would rise there and we would shoot the nets around, using the two boats. One boat would go out on a half circle and the other would shoot on the other side. You'd catch them in one net and pull it in towards the beach until it was like a horseshoe. You'd pull the net aboard the big boat. The big boat had the net the fish went into or were tucked in, as we say, and the smaller boat had a net which was more or less a stop-gap, to cut across the end of the space so the fish couldn't get out again. There were usually five men in the big boat and three or four in the small one. You could catch three or four tons of fish on a trip. I started early getting my experience. At that time I was what you might call a schoolboy fisherman; I was learning at school and learning at sea.

We'd go out at the break of day, about three o'clock in the morning. The fish would start to rise as soon as daylight dawned, and we'd see them starting to jump. It was quiet then and you could get the net round them easily. Later in the day when the sun was shining and they were on the move travelling hard, if we didn't shoot the net across the way they were going, we wouldn't catch them. We had to get the net across their noses because we couldn't shoot it as fast as they were going. In the early morning, before they were on the move, in a good shoal of herring you might count ten thousand. We were usually home for breakfast by eight o'clock.

The mackerel season used to start in June and last through July and August into September; they would go away after that. The mackerel would feed during those months on very small herrings. When the mackerel went away we would put our nets aboard the big boats for drifting for pilchards. Then we would bait lines to catch whiting. Some seasons we might cut out the pilchards and concentrate on the whiting or the other way round. For whiting you'd have a thousand hooks on a line using mackerel as bait. Six stones of mackerel would be laid out the night before. Then we'd go down at three o'clock in the morning, take those mackerel aboard and if there were four men, three would be cutting them up for bait as we sailed out to the fishing ground, maybe taking an hour and a half or more. The fourth man was steering. We'd put the kettle on for a cup of tea and shoot the lines, say three miles. Then we would go back to the other end of the lines, when three of the men would be down below having their cup of tea and one would be steering. Then we'd start pulling; one would be hauling, another man would be taking off the fish, and the other two would be starting to bait the line again. We'd come back into harbour, have our dinner, go back down to the boat and go out again, finishing the baiting of the line on the way out and maybe fishing from three to five o'clock in the afternoon. We did different kinds of fishing at different times.

There were three fish buyers in Mevagissey. There was Robbins who was local, Pawlyn who had stores also at Padstow, Porthleven and Plymouth, and a Mr Edwards who had a store over on the West Quay, which has now been made into cafés. All those stores are now gone.

When we brought the fish in they were washed in big tubs. They had boxes each side of the tubs and they'd pack them in the boxes and then ice them. They'd nail the covers on and stack them up ready to go to the station and catch the midday or afternoon train to Billingsgate or elsewhere.

In those days the fishermen got about a shilling a stone. It was the buyers and fish merchants who made the real profits. I'll never forget when I started the job of fishing and got paid for it. I had left school at fourteen and in April 1917 I went out. There were three of us with nets and there was no engine in the little boat. We were about fourteen miles off shore, with a fine breeze blowing and with the sails up we were going as fast as a motor boat. We pulled in the nets about midnight, but the wind was coming off Mevagissey so we couldn't go in because with an off shore wind the sails were no use to us. So, as we had oars, we rowed from midnight till eight in the morning, when we came into harbour – that was some night. Big boats with motors could come straight into Mevagissey, but because of the wind we had to row first in the direction of the Lizard, then come up towards Fowey, then come back down to row into Mevagissey.

Another time just after I left school, I and another boy were fishing with an older man who owned the boat. We caught some herring and we lads each got a share of £1.13s.6d. That was a sovereign, half-a-sovereign, half-a-crown and a bob. The other boy who was a bit older than me said he would keep three and six for himself and give his mother thirty bob. I thought I'd keep half-a-crown and give my mother thirty-one shillings. When I got home it was dinner time, so I put the thirty-one shillings on the table. There were eight including myself round the table; my father and mother, four sisters and a brother. My mother said, 'That boy's got a week's living for all eight of us. Keep a shilling to yourself'. Like a fool I said, 'I don't want it.' She was suspicious at once. 'You don't want a shilling?' she says. 'No,' I said, 'I got half-a-crown.' 'What,' she said, 'half-a-crown? I can buy so much flour and lard and make pastry and bread for all eight of us for a week. What would you do with half-a-crown?' She had a good mind to take away the shilling as well as the half crown – and I had to promise not to throw it away on sweets and things before she would allow me to keep the shilling. My mother had to take in washing t help feed us all when fishing was slack. That's what it was like in those days; every penny counted.

I could have gone to grammar school but my father wanted me to go fishing. I was in the seventh standard at school in Mevagissey for four years. I actually moved up each class every six months instead of every twelve months. I seemed to be able to do the work without trouble. But there were my four sisters to keep and they were hard times. So I became a fisherman, for every little bit extra helped.

Somebody asked me what we did in the early days with our leisure time. There was no leisure time. When we weren't at sea, we were up in the lofts mending or making our equipment or gear. I learned not just how to use nets but also how to make them. Just recently I was demonstrating at a church fair. A lady visitor had been watching me making a net and asked me if she could have a go. I showed her how and she was very pleased at having made a bit of fishing net. She felt her visit to Mevagissey had been that bit more interesting. The lofts above the houses were full of nets in those days. There were herring nets, pilchard nets, mackerel nets, ray nets and also whiting lines and dog lines which were middle lines; the dogfish would eat through fine lines. Long lines big as your finger were for fish like conger and ling and skate, and we'd shoot maybe seven or eight miles of line when we were line fishing. We'd have baskets of lines with hooks that went round a cork. When the line was clear you'd put the bait on and you'd shoot the lines out from one basket after another. You'd tie the line at the bottom end of one basket to the top end of the next one. You had to keep going. You'd put down your marker first, then your grafer (a small anchor), just to hold the line on the bottom. After a few hours, we used a little hand winch called the iron man to pull up the lines, then later we had the motor winches. This was for the big lines. The same applied to the whiting fine lines. Then the men who weren't doing anything else would be clearing the baskets and sticking hooks right round the cork ready for baiting again.

In any spare time we did the mending of the nets and lines in the lofts. My brother and I would make the lines and nets ourselves. We used white cotton but that had to be cured two or three times, with cutch which made it brown. Then we'd put it in a bath of warm tar two or three times. They use cat gut now. A firm at Bridport makes all sorts of nets; trawl nets and all. In the early days looking after and making nets left no time for leisure.

There was a lot of manual work when I started both in the

21

lofts and on the boats. We had a lot of dragging and pulling nets and twice I've had operations for hernia. My father suffered from it and so did my grandfather, but there were no operations for them; they wore trusses. Yes, in those days fishermen had hard lives with not a great return for all their hard work. Nowadays they've more machinery to help them, but at that time the fishermen made the poorest living and the buyers took the biggest share.

I'll tell you a story about profits. We had been working ray nets, with nets on the bottom, seven or eight feet deep, and leads on the bottom rope, corks on the top. We'd been six or seven miles out with thirty or forty nets. We'd caught ray and turbot and monkfish, crab and lobster. We'd pulled them up every four or five days when the weather was suitable and we'd sold them all to the same buyer. One afternoon we landed forty-six stone of turbot and were paid four pence halfpenny a stone. That same Saturday evening my brother was up at St Austell where the buyer had a fish shop. He could see the turbot we'd caught in the window. The man in the shop saw him looking at them and he came out and said, 'Would you like some turbot, gov'nor? We're selling them off cheap to clear them as it's Saturday night. One and six per pound; that's cheap'. There had been no labour involved for the buyer because we'd gutted them. You can see we had to catch a lot of fish to make a living.

Fishing was what kept Mevagissey going. The wives were involved in it too. When the pilchards were landed, they salted them in tanks. Where the car park is now was a building with big tanks. The pilchards were thrown in the tanks and salted till the tank was full. After three weeks they were taken out and the women would pack them in barrels, round and round, till they had them right up to the top. They'd screw them down to press the oil out. Then they'd fill them up again till the barrel wouldn't hold any more. The barrels were exported to Italy. It was a thriving industry in those days.

Every penny that came into the house was needed. When I was about thirty years of age and married I was getting thirty bob a week. But all wages then were low. For instance, a skilled shipwright from the yard who came to do a job on a boat got only £1 a week and that was after six years' apprenticeship. So if we got thirty bob a week, we were getting more than a tradesman.

My father and his brother owned a boat and when they died I took it over. Then I saved up to have a new twenty-two foot boat with 7ft beam and a 7h.p. engine built. That cost me £45; nowadays when you're talking about a new boat, you're talking about hundreds or thousands of pounds.

Cornwall's coast can be treacherous, specially with the rocks. I remember one near miss we had in a fog, although it was as much the run of the tide as the fog that caused it. Instead of coming into the bay we came onto the rocks round the point. On the deck we had twenty-seven boxes full of fish and as the boat started to roll the boxes broke loose and slid and rolled across the deck. We stopped one engine and the propeller was grinding on the rocks, then we stopped the other engine and the same thing happened. We took out the oar and pushed against the rocks. Anything might have happened, but suddenly the boat slid off the rocks and we managed to crawl round into harbour. That was a lucky escape.

We used two boats, the big forty foot lugger which almost went on the rocks in the fog and a small twenty-four foot boat for inshore. We worked them alternately, laying off one at a time. We used the lugger for drift nets – whiting, ray, dogfish, herring and so on. The small boat was used for the shoals of mackerel near the shore. The mackerel would come in to feed on the small fish. We seldom got herring in this area. We had to go up to the Plymouth area for the herring. We'd stay up there in the boat and come home to Mevagissey by bus at the weekends. One year herring did come down here after dawn every day and we got 700 stone. We had small boats loaded down with them. This only lasted about a fortnight. We got three shillings a stone at that time. The buyer made such profit he got a new lorry out of it. We used to call it the herring lorry.

The price we got for our herring suddenly shot down because of something that happened. There was a man up at Pentewan who pulled his boat right onto the beach and sold his catch unwashed with all the shells and dirt. They looked a sorry sight and he had to sell them cheap. This affected the price we could get. We had started off in the morning by getting ten

OC—C

shillings a hundred herring (120 we used to say). Then in the afternoon we were only getting five shillings a hundred. In the evening they put them down to three shillings. The thing was the buyer had lowered the price for the mucky fish at Pentewan so the Mevagissey buyer lowered his price as well and got our good fish for the cheaper rate. We just couldn't win.

Apart from the weather, we had another kind of danger during the war. When the war started I was thirty-nine so I went on with the fishing. I was working then with two young chaps. It was tricky at night for we couldn't use the lights and had to make do with a lantern when we were drifting for herring or pilchards. Once, when we were out hauling our nets there would have been less than a quarter of a mile separating the fishing boats, I heard the rattle of machine guns but I didn't at first pay any attention because I had often heard our airmen at practice, one plane towing a target and another plane firing at it. I heard this plane but I was sitting meshing so I didn't take much notice until suddenly the plane was right above the boat. I happened to look up and saw the German black cross on it just as he started firing, but the plane was just past us and we could see the bullets ploughing along the water. He hit the boat next to ours and the four men on it just went down and seemed to vanish. Bullets struck the block on the mast and down came the sail. I thought the men had all been killed, but a few seconds later up they got and cut away their nets and made for harbour. I remember the fishery officer from Falmouth came to question the men. 'What did you do when the bullets hit the boat?' he asked. 'Oh, we lished, mister.' That's the word fishermen use when you're shooting and a shoal of fish go down deeper in the sea!

Since the war the number of fishing boats has gone down. There are only about three of the forty-footers left. Nowadays they fish for ray and ling and pollack; they shoot their nets out on the wrecks, but they can only do it when the tides are quiet. They've got their charts and with the help of the echo-sounder they can locate the wrecks, for the fish live in them and around them. The fishermen know exactly where a steamer is lying and they shoot their nets, gill nets, right alongside her. Pollack and ling and cod all live in the wrecks. The tide has to be quiet or a dead tide as we call it, because if it's running hard as at spring tides, when they're pulling the net will catch in the steamer and tear away because of the derricks and masts lying about. The fishermen come every fortnight when the moon is full. Trawlers can't work where the wrecks are because they'd lose their trawl. But the big boats use gill nets beside the wrecks because they can pull them away.

Fishing has gone downhill in these last years. Stocks of fish are less, although small boats using ground nets still catch some fish like monk and ray and there are a few crabbers. Scottish trawlermen have depleted the mackerel and small ones are unsaleable and have to be thrown overboard. In the summer fishermen take visitors out fishing but in the winter there's not much for them to do.

My son went to Birmingham University on a scholarship where he took a BA, then an MA and went on to Oxford to take his teaching diploma. My grandson has now gone to university. Fishing at one time was a family industry but young folk are moving away from it.

TOMMY MORRISSEY

My father was a fisherman in Padstow all his life. It's a life that has dangers but you've got to learn to cope with them. As a boy I learned about the sea, especially the dangers around this coast, through sailing with my father who owned his own boat.

The Doom Bar at the entrance to the Camel estuary is a drawback to Padstow. There's a big groundswell from the heavy seas piling in from the western ocean, fifteen to twenty feet high, pounding up there when the weather is really bad and you get a big surf.

I'd heard stories from my father like the tragedy that happened on 11th April, 1900. It involved three boats and many lives. A boat called the *Peace and Plenty* got into trouble on the Bar. The *Arab*, our rowing lifeboat, went out to help her, but it was so bad that the *Arab* itself got into difficulties. Then the *James Stevenson*, our first steam lifeboat, went out after their pals but she was driven over to the cave half way between Greenaway and Polzeath. The engineers on the *James Stevenson* were battened down and they couldn't get out. The coxswain and his son were drowned, but three of the lifeboat crew got off the *James Stevenson* and swam to safety across the estuary. The *Peace and Plenty* itself was wrecked and all its crew were drowned. The crew of the *Arab* were luckier; they all got out of their boat and managed to get ashore across the estuary at Daymer Bay.

Over the years I learned to deal with dangerous conditions. You must be aware of possible danger, sudden squalls or gales coming up. If you keep your boat and your engine in good order you've a better chance. I've always done every job that needed to be done to look after a boat. In those early days boats weren't large, maybe up to twenty-four foot on average, and they had low-powered engines. But there was one great thing. No matter if there were personal differences, we'd always help each other if there was trouble, if nets got stuck on propellors or in storms. Even your biggest enemy would push up alongside and offer you a tow.

Last century Padstow had both fishing and boat building. There were five yards building boats. Harry Cowl was a famous builder. His uncle built the yacht my father raced. He also built some wonderful sailing ships from the 1860s. When I was a boy the largest boat I saw that was built in Padstow was the old barge, the *Beaumaris,* built by Steve Brabyn. His yard was where the Waterside Flats are now; above was the ice-factory and underneath the boat yard. But all that has gone. There is no boat building. There is only fishing.

As a boy I started fishing with my father who had bought a four-masted barque called the *Antoinette*. It had been wrecked on the bar. My father put a Kelvin engine from Glasgow in it and when I took it over in 1929 I put another engine in it. When I went after herring I'd have a crew of two besides myself.

I worked hard and made a good living. One week we started at midnight Sunday and we never pulled our sea boots off till midnight Friday. Usually we'd go out in the afternoon and shoot the nets as evening was coming on, at the swim of the moon as it was rising. You had to watch out for the signs of the herring, for remember there were no aids then, no sounders, no radar. You'd maybe see a basking shark swimming after the herring shoals that were feeding on plankton, or the gannets

26

and gulls wheeling around. You got to know the signs.

In those early days as the seasons came round, the pattern of fishing was the same year by year. In the spring and onwards there was the inshore fishing for lobsters, crab and crayfish. From the middle of October till the middle of January was the herring season.

In 1938 I bought the *Girl Maureen*. She had been a lifeboat and was sent over here to replace our lifeboat which had been lost at St Ives. The *Girl Maureen* became redundant and someone bought her to make her into a yacht and I bought her off him. I fished from her for thirty-two years. *Girl Maureen* was a double-ender; that is, she had two sharp bow ends, not a square stern. She was self-righting and as she had been designed for rowing she had no engine, like the old lifeboats which you could use in surf and beach or take over bars. You didn't need to pull her out before turning her round. When she was a lifeboat she was launched to rescue a wreck being towed round to Pembroke for breaking up. I worked on her and turned her into a fishing boat.

In 1982 I let the *Girl Maureen* go to the museum in Lynmouth. It was a good thing for now this type of old lifeboat will be preserved for later generations to see. She replaced the *Louisa*, a sister ship which had been hauled across Exmoor in a rescue bid.

Since I was a boy I wanted to be a fisherman and there are lads in Padstow who have the sea in their blood. Over the years a lot of them have been with me. They began by pulling and sculling our dinghies, as the lads still do. They still start as I did before they leave school. There's a little boy with me now; every weekend, when the tide's in, he's down with me rowing the dinghy round the quay. He just can't keep away. He has started going out crabbing with me much to the amusement of everyone. If you're going to handle a small boat it's better and safer to be brought up to it. It's not the same even if you go into the Navy or the Merchant Navy. When they drop down to our class of work with a small boat, they find it's quite different. You've got to be brought up to this particular kind of seamanship.

Several young chaps who served their time with me have their own boats and are doing well. From Padstow now, in the mid-1980s, there are fourteen full-time fishing boats and three over on the other side of the estuary at Rock.

In the nineteen-thirties fishing and the fish market were the important things in Padstow, and herring was the money spinner. There weren't the same number of visitors or tourists in those days. The few who came with their families would bring their staff or servants and maybe stay for two months. There were very few motor cars, just a few around the quay.

Although there was quite a bit of unemployment most men found seasonal jobs, for instance in the fish market or on the dock working on the cargoes of the coasters. The fish market took in a number from January till May when the boats were fishing all round this area. They would work from Padstow up to the 'Obby 'Oss festival on the 1st May. Then some boats would leave Padstow for Fleetwood and fish in Morecombe Bay.

I would lay up my boat for a few months and work for another company's boat. Then the company's boat would leave Padstow after the 'Obby 'Oss festival to go back to its home port of Yarmouth. I'd stay at home in Padstow and get on with fishing here. The Yarmouth boats would be refitted as drifters and then do the northern voyage to Scotland.

This way I made a good living and we were never short of money. The pattern of fishing may be much the same as it was then, except for the disappearance of the herring. But one thing that has changed is the value of different kinds of fish. It has made the fishing nowadays better in some ways. I suppose it's due to changes in what people like to eat, changes in taste. It's chiefly shell fish that the fishermen here go for now. There's a big market for that. You don't find much netting for pollack, hake and so on. Take the case of spider crabs. In the old days we couldn't sell spider crabs and we couldn't sell squid or monk fish – we had to shovel them back overboard. These three fish now, crab, squid and monk, are making fantastic money. There are boats from Scotland landing £50,000 to £60,000 worth of squid after four or five days work in the Rockall area. And all that was shovelled overboard when we were fishing. It was rubbish then. We'd throw away seven or eight hundredweight of spider crabs day after day. Now they're fetching over £1 a kilo. We'd pull a few toes off them and keep

28

them for the old age pensioners who'd come down to get them. The rubbish we threw away, that's where the gold is now.

Another way fishing is different is because of the use of aids, also the cost of buying a boat and all the fishing gear. If you buy your boat through the White Fish Authority, there is their loan and grant scheme, for which you get a 30 per cent grant. You put 15 per cent down and the rest is borrowed on loan for five, ten, or fifteen years. That's how fishermen today must start, for a young man could never afford a boat costing £20,000 without the loan and grant scheme. In my young days you could buy a boat for £5 and a second-hand engine for £5.

Nowadays when you're a commercial fisherman you must fish to the limit to pay back loans and grants and you must have every modern aid, like Decca Navigators, radar and sonar. It isn't likely you can buy it outright, so it has to be rented. The Decca can be over £1,000 a year to rent.

You make yourself a slave if you go in for that type of modern fishing in a bigger boat. In my own boat I had just an echo-sounder and VHF radio. That was nothing really and of course I owned the boat. I had no expenses bar the fuel and harbour dues. If you're working a bigger boat nowadays you can hardly even afford to tie up to the wall. It all depends on the kind of boat and the kind of fisherman you want to be.

I made every repair to my gear and boat and engine myself. Many nowadays couldn't cope with my kind of one-man fishing. They've not been brought up to deal with everything. They're dealing with gadgets all the time, but don't mistake me, they're damn good men. They've got to be to make it pay. It's an entirely different way of working and fishing. On a modern boat if you rip a net, it's thrown on shore and sent to a repairer. You get maintenance engineers on board as soon as you tie up. The skipper and crew just go off. Their job has been to get as much fish as possible – quantity's the thing. And nowadays the sad thing is most of it goes for meal and manure and not for the table. You get different types of fishermen. There are still blokes like me who'd rather be on their own or maybe with a mate in a small boat, for inshore work, who do every job that needs to be done. We all have our own way of doing things.

Nowadays every morning I go out in a little boat to catch mackerel. Since I retired from making my living by fishing, it's what I enjoy and it helps to keep me occupied. But I do other things. You've heard of the two 'Osses that take part in the 'Obby 'Oss festival each May. Well, I've looked after one for ten years and the other for fifty-two years. I make them up, paint them and renovate them for each festival. It's the Peace horse, the Blue Ribbon 'Oss I've done for fifty-two years. My uncle put me in charge of that one. I suppose I got the job of painting the two heads just because I offered. Most people like the fun, not the work side of it. When I give it up somebody will take it on. My daughter is as keen as mustard. She's seen it done so many times, she's all for it. In Padstow the tradition of the 'Obby 'Oss will never die out.

Another activity I've got is making small models of ships and putting them in glass bottles. I've got one here that's mounted on a piece of driftwood. It's a three-masted barque. I made it in about a week. You put putty and paint in the bottle. That's a base to hold the ship steady when you put it in. You've got to let the paint and putty dry and harden. Then you pull the masts upright with strings attached to them. There were twenty-one moving ends on that one, strings attached to it. You hear people say it can be done by pulling one string but you can't. I send these bottles all over the world – China, Peru, India. I've got five on order now from a lady in California. I've got to get the five bottles first but I'd like them full of whisky!

I've done all the paintings of ships on the walls of my sitting-room. There's one of the *Katie* that came to take the place of the *James Stevenson*, the first steam lifeboat, and one of the *Girl Maureen* and others. There's plenty to keep me busy.

One of the interesting things about my life in Padstow as a fisherman has been the number of well-known people I've taken out sailing. My father started it and after he gave it up they came with me. Many learned their sailing here. I remember the time Ali Khan gave me a tip of £20, which was quite a sum in those days. I asked him if he hadn't made a mistake but he had not. I taught quite a number of notable people over the years. One chap later won the Fastnet race. Max Aitken of the Daily Express spent a lot of time here and I took him out. I used to sail with Viscount Clifden of Lanhydrock and his two sisters, the Hon. Everilda and the Hon. Violet Agar-Robartes. In 1934 when I was in hospital with appendicitis they visited me every week and brought fruit and chocolate. I also took the Duchess of Kent and her children sailing and Captain Mark Phillips, Princess Anne's husband. All sorts of people are drawn to the sea and get great pleasure from it.

I remember taking out an old gentleman named Carruthers. He had two fingers missing from his right hand. He had been an extra master under sail on a big four-master from the river Elbe to Iquique, in the north of Chile, and back, with fertilisers and sulphates. When he came aboard I had the engine running. He said 'You're another sailor whose got all the sails but doesn't use them.' I said 'I'll put the sails up if you want them.' So I put the sails up and we sailed all round. He showed me his fingers. 'Look at that,' he said, 'I got this through knocking a pin out of an anchor on a windjammer when I was an apprentice.' When we were coming in, he said 'You can take the sails down and start the engine.' 'No way,' I retorted; 'You wanted to sail; we sail, no engine'.

We became great friends after that. He had sailing in his blood, and so had I.

WALTER BOYD, B E M

Trinity House Officer

In 1983 Walter Boyd was awarded the BEM for the outstanding part he played in furthering the coastal services around Cornwall for almost half a century. This is part of the citation: 'His duties involved him in the organisation of the regular helicopter relief of Round Island, Longships, Bishop Rock lighthouses and Seven Stones Lightvessel. He devotes time to lecturing school parties in the work of Trinity House. Deputy Master Sir Miles Wingate says, "Mr Boyd's record for the past 48 years has been one of exemplary loyal and faithful service in the various positions which he has held. His outstanding dedication to duty over and above that expected of him has set an exceptional example to the many Trinity House personnel who have come into contact with him" '.

My father was master of the Seven Stones Lightship. My brother joined the Marines. But when I became old enough, I worked in a grocery store for nine months at five shillings a week.

Then one day Father said to me, 'There's a job going aboard the ship at twenty-five shillings a week. If you come down and get it, don't let me down. If you let me down, I'll kick your bottom for you.' So away I went and got the job as boy. Later I was made assistant steward; I was on three years' probation, even though the job was permanent.

I spent all the war years, including the Normandy landings, doing buoyage work throughout the Western Approaches, that is the laying of buoys along the swept channels for the convoys to go through. All this work was under the direction of Trinity House. I carried on with Trinity House in the steam vessel service until 1957. After twenty-four years at sea I came ashore.

I worked ashore in the stores at Penzance. In 1966 I was given the job of Wharf Bosun, in charge of our depot at

Penzance, involving supervising staff and buoyage and everything connected with these operations. In those days we had a permanent ship here, the *Stella*. We also loaded ships for Trinity House which had, I think, nine ships round the coast. There was a depot at Great Yarmouth. Harwich was the main district depot. We had workshops and headquarters in London at Tower Hill. Cowes in the Isle of Wight was another depot, also Penzance, Swansea and Holyhead. Each one had a ship and some had two ships, whose job was to maintain buoyage, service the light-vessels, and supply lighthouses with such necessities as oil, water and provisions. If there were breakdowns, we'd send mechanics or electricians where they were needed.

In the early seventies, Trinity House decided they were going to use helicopters to carry out some of the work. They started off down here with a helipad on the Wolf Rock, about nine miles off Land's End. It turned out to be a success, but the helicopters they were using then, Bristow's Wessex, were too heavy to land on the pad. So what we had to do was load all the stores in the helicopter, which would then hover say a couple of feet from the deck while the men and stores were lowered onto the pad. I think that continued for about eighteen months until another firm took the contracts. It is still the same firm today although the name is changed. In those days it was known as Management Aviation. Recently they've changed their name to Bond Helicopters. They started off with lighter, smaller helicopters which could land on helipads. (When I retired this firm presented me with a beautiful inscribed model.) Next they put a pad on the Round Island lighthouse and the Longships lighthouse. The helicopters were now able to land on all the rock lighthouses we had down here – Wolf, Round Island, the Bishop Rock and the Scillies – they all eventually had pads and also the lightships were fitted with helipads. Down here we have such heavy ground swell that landing is sometimes very tricky. The skill of the pilots is fantastic. They are unsurpassed at landing on a rolling deck as they do. They all had navy training but the Bond twin brothers, Mike and Geoff, whose father started their helicopter company, Management Aviation, are skilled civilian pilots. I'd go anywhere and do anything with them.

A lighthouse keeper used to do two months on the lighthouse and one month ashore. In the days before the helicopter, men and supplies would go in by boat. The boat would go in as close as possible and the men would put their foot in a bowline and be winched up. Of course the helicopters cut that out. But at that time it was possible for a man to do over a hundred days on a rock, an awful long time.

All the navigation aids and all the lights round the coast of England and Wales are the responsibility of Trinity House. Scotland comes under the Northern Lighthouse Board. Some ports, like Liverpool and Falmouth, maintain their own local lights, on piers and so on, and some provide their own local buoyage on estuaries, but that is just local. Seaward work is all Trinity House.

I was in charge of the stores; the paints, cleaning materials, ropes, and all supplies like machinery parts going out. Later, as wharf bosun I was responsible for maintaining all the buoys, including cleaning and checking the chains, and sinkers. We had to check them for the lighting and get them ready for the change-over and also meet the ships' requirements when they came in.

When the helicopters came to be more succesful, we had a base at Sennen, about ten miles from Penzance, where we built our own small heliport where the helicopters could be refuelled. We had radio and fire-fighting equipment there and other necessary equipment, all of which I was in charge of. To begin with the helicopters only came once a month then it became every fortnight. So every other week we were working a helicopter.

We'd fill up hundred gallon butyl tanks and undersling them on the helicopters. In that way we could supply the lighthouses all round Land's End with oil and water. At first we couldn't make it to the Scillies; they weren't worried at Round Island for it's quite a big island and they could store a lot of fuel and water there but the Bishop Rock was a bit awkward. By then some of the ships had helicopter platforms fitted to them, so they could be supplied too. I went over to St Mary's airport in the Scillies in 1958 and we put together the fittings, with the cooperation of the airport, that would fit on to our butyl tanks.

We could put five bags of water, about ninety-five gallons in each, into the Longships lighthouse off Land's End, in eighteen minutes from the time the helicopter took off. A journey to the Wolf Rock and back took eleven and a half minutes from the time the helicopter left Sennen.

The result of all these developments with the helicopters is that now Trinity House has reduced their fleet of boats to the *Patricia*, the *Stella*, the *Winston Churchill* and the *Mermaid*; I think just four left from about nine.

When they took over helicopters first there was one, then they had two. All the lightships were relieved by helicopters. One would do the east coast and the other would do the west coast. Once a fortnight the helicopters would get back to their base at Strubby in Lincolnshire. A helicopter would set out from there to Holyhead in North Wales at the beginning of the week. It would do what was required in that area. Then later in that week, it would go on and do what was needed in the Swansea and Bristol Channel area. Then it would be down here on the following Sunday or Monday and perhaps work here till Tuesday or Wednesday morning. Then off it would go to the Channel Islands. On Thursday it would do the south coast from Shoreham and from there return to Strubby.

The second helicopter would be sent with a relief pilot and engineer towards the end of the first week, so the pilot would be relieved at Swansea. The relieving pilot would complete the circuit and take his helicopter back to Strubby. The helicopters would take turns at the different routes. They alternated them because the one that did the east coast didn't do nearly as much work as the west coast helicopter.

My own responsibilities increased with all the helicopter developments. I was always the bosun of the yard but when the flying got more important, perhaps on Sunday, Monday and Tuesday I'd be at Sennen. I was in charge of personnel going away and coming ashore, and of their transport into Penzance. I would tell the pilot what stores he had to take and work out everybody's weights, and deal with radio matters. I got my own radio-operator's certificate. I was also in charge of first aid. I did first aid courses, fire-fighting courses and flight-deck training with the Navy at Portland. I also went to the Merchant Navy Officers' School at Greenhythe near Gravesend and then went on survival courses. This included learning what to do if an aircraft ditched, how to get into life rafts, righting life rafts at sea, dealing with hypothermia and survival and that sort of thing.

About five years before I retired it was decided to fit all personnel out with survival suits. I used to give them a pre-flight briefing because the helicopter engineers were very pushed for time. I'd get them into their survival suits and instruct them what to do and what not to do when they entered the helicopter. As I said, I'd arrange the loads in conjunction with the pilot and I'd see them off.

I'm glad to say that never in all those years, and I was forty-eight and a half years with Trinity House, was I involved in a tragedy in my sphere of work. Occasionally people would do silly things, like loosening their belts when the helicopter was just coming in to land, but the engineer would spot their movements in his mirror and he would give them hell. Outside of that we never had an accident in this part of the world. Sometimes accidents outside my own sphere, such as the tragedy of the Penlee lifeboat, would affect me. After the tragedy they called me and asked for a safe place where they could store wreckage that was being brought in. I went down with the police and looked after a lot of the wreckage, life-jackets and so on. Everything that was found came into our place and I looked after it for the Lifeboat Institution. I got many appreciative letters, including one from the chief of operations from the lifeboats.

I've known our pilots do reliefs of lighthouses in gale force winds up to forty-five knots, landing on the rocks. The only thing that would stop them would be very heavy fog. Sometimes the heavy sea would come up over the helipad of, say, Wolf Rock and the pilot would have to watch out.

I was blessed that my long experience fell in with all the developments of Trinity House service in and around Cornwall. I've been a part of it. We had come to the point with the terrific seas on this coast that the boats had reached the limit of what they could achieve in supplying the lighthouses. The helicopter revolution had to come.

In 1952 I was picked to go on a six week trip with the Duke of Edinburgh's party on the *Patricia* to the Olympic Games in

Finland. She was one of the five survivors of the nine Trinity House ships at the end of the war, the other four having been lost by enemy action. We went first to Oslo where we had ten days. The Norwegian royal family came aboard for dinner. We had another ten days at Helsingbord in Sweden, then we went up to Helsinki in Finland. The members of the Scandinavian royal families and ambassadors would come aboard for an evening. After a fortnight in Finland we came back down the Baltic again. General Browning, Daphne du Maurier's husband, was with us. He was aide to the Duke of Edinburgh, who was the Grand Master of Trinity House. Many sailors lost their lives during the *Patricia's* war time service.

FRANK POOLEY

PC 203

I joined the Royal Engineers at the age of seventeen and when I was nineteen I joined the Cornish Police, nearly seventy years ago. I began at headquarters in Bodmin. Places like Truro and Penzance had their own police forces but then the whole lot got amalgamated. Now of course, Cornwall and Devon are one.

I did my early training at Bodmin. A history of the Cornwall Constabulary was published at the time of the centenary celebrations. It brought back many memories to me, and it gives fascinating glimpses of the earliest days.

Our own County Police Force was established in 1857. There was some opposition to this move for fear of a rise in the rates. However they advertised and filled the post of chief constable. They gave the job to Colonel Walter Raleigh Elbert at a salary of £350 a year plus £100 for expenses. We've only had four chief constables since then.

The first chief constable was a very active man and recruited on visits to places like St Austell and Truro. He reported that he had selected six divisions for occupation, in preference to distributing the present small force around the county, with a view to drawing a cordon on the Devonshire side and thus preventing as much as possible the ingress of tramps and vagrants, and also of rendering the escape of offenders more difficult. A lot of people wanted more police in the west of the county to prevent vagrants entering by boat at Hayle.

The very first constable, PC 1, was a Bodmin man. He had a top hat, great coat and cape. He had one pair of handcuffs, a stout staff, lantern and knapsack. It took fourteen years before the top hat gave way to the helmet. About that time permission was given to grow a moustache.

Since those early days there hasn't been a great deal of difference in types of crimes but there certainly has been in the methods of dealing with them and in attitudes to criminals. Not long before the new force was established a man had been hanged for stealing a sheep. Then the penalty became transportation for twenty years. Boys in their early teens went to prison for hawking without a licence. You could get two months in prison for stealing some horse-hair and ten days' hard labour for wandering about without a job. If you were drunk you'd be put in the stocks.

My training in Bodmin was different from the hard training of the earliest recruits. They were put through military manoeuvres three times a day in a yard at the back of the police office in Castle Street. I had to learn the police book of regulations, and how to deal with cases. They were short of constables on the beat then and wanted to get recruits out as quickly as possible, so I only had seven weeks' training before going on duty.

I gained experience at Tregony and Falmouth. At Falmouth at that time there were a superintendent, two sergeants and several constables. There were the usual things to do: drunks to be taken to the cells till they were sensible again, accidents to be attended to, sudden deaths and taking part in inquests, and making enquiries if a crime was committed. Murders were few and far between and I never was actually involved in a case. But there was a bad one over at St Austell when a lad murdered his father and mother and tipped their bodies over a cliff, in the 1950s.

You had to go wherever you were sent. I was sent to St Ives, then to Camborne, then back to St Ives where I met and married a local girl. We've been married now for forty-five years. We hadn't much money but we got along. When I first joined in 1919 I got ten shillings a week but soon after the war finished the pay was raised to three guineas (£3.3s.0d.) a week. I was lucky, for the rise was backdated to before I joined, so I was due a nice bit of back pay. After twenty-two years' service with the force I was getting £4.15s.0d. as a constable. Promotion was slow in those days. Each of the five county divisions had a superintendent.

There were two distinct areas in St Ives, the Downalong and the Upalong. The Downalong was the area beside the water and the beach and harbour where the fisherman operated. The Upalong was the area higher up. The fishermen had strong

OC—D

39

religious beliefs. They wouldn't allow anyone to take a boat out on a Sunday. Nobody could do any kind of work on the beach on a Sunday, no painting of boats nor anything like that. My wife's grandfather was a fish buyer who had worked right at the beginning of the century. His family knew everybody. We have an old photograph of her grandfather taken in 1906, standing among the women who worked for him. They're counting the herrings going into the barrels. They counted the fish in lots of a hundred, but really it was 120. Horses and carts would take the herring barrels round to the railway station. Grandfather would follow the herring fishermen round the coast of Britain to Scotland and Northern Ireland.

My wife's family lived in the Upalong, and she remembers the days when there was always a policeman around when the herring were being put in the barrels. There was great activity all round the harbour. In those days there wasn't much crime. Everybody knew each other and the kind of person they were. If anything happened, the policeman would know which house to go to. There were the rogues but we knew who they were. At that time the people in St Ives wouldn't have dreamed of locking their doors when they went to bed.

In 1926 I was one of the police sent up from Cornwall to the West Riding of Yorkshire for the coal strike. We never had any of the clashes with pickets you have seen recently on television. The strikers just kept out of the way. It was mostly thieving, there wasn't the marching and so on. We kept an eye on the mine shafts. The miners would throw coal out of the trucks and come back later and pick it up in sacks. We tried to prevent that. Four sergeants and twenty-six constables were sent from the county. Before my time a contingent of police were sent down to Cornwall from Wales to help in keeping order during the strike in the clay industry in 1913. They were there to prevent damage being done. It's not a new thing, police being sent from one part of the country to another.

The police service has changed in several ways. It was more personal in those days, especially in the villages, where you were in your own station. Everybody with a problem came to the policeman; they would even come with their family troubles. You were a part of the community. That's why I liked village life. You were your own boss, and you knew your parish.

40

When you were in a village your wife had to look after the telephone when you were out. You walked around and talked to everybody; we didn't have police cars. The residents were in touch with us. As the years went on I was sent to Penryn and to the village of Mawnan Smith. We enjoyed it there. Our two children were born there and we were loath to leave it when we had to move on.

The Second World War found us at Wadebridge where I had the duties of keeping an eye on the blackout and dealing with the usual petty offences. During the blitz I had to go to Plymouth. I helped to look after the properties that had been damaged. Their occupants had to get into the country while we watched over their properties.

Later we went to the village of Blisland where my wife even had the job of signing on the Home Guard! We'd joke about her being an unpaid member of the force. I would be on night duty and in the middle of the night my wife would have to take an emergency call from London. There had been a big burglary and the information had to be circulated quickly round the country. So there she was, shivering in her nightdress and taking down all the details to hand to me when I came off duty. Not only that; she had to phone the details to the next station. Somebody always had to be there to answer the phone. I suppose that's why man and wife teams were important in country places. At country stations like Blisland the policeman also had work connected with farming. I was on duty at the sheep dipping, or if there was an outbreak of foot-and-mouth I had to make sure the regulations were kept and everything was disinfected. I also had to stop anybody who was not strictly on business from coming on to a farm where there was the disease. The lives of a village policeman and of a town policeman were quite different.

In 1942 I was back in Bodmin again. Bodmin was a changed place during the war. For one thing we had the Americans in the Duke of Cornwall's Light Infantry's barracks. In the fields up above they built their huts. Their own military police did the patrolling up there. It was only when they came down into the town that it affected us. The Americans brought a lot of money to the area and that meant a lot of women were attracted to the town, and as with any big

41

number of men there are always a few who might step out of line. When I first started in the police Bodmin was a different sort of place. You didn't get the vandalism and hooliganism you get now but you did get drunks to deal with. During the war there was a bit of theft. The post office was broken into, so was a hotel. The Americans were noisy and sometimes a bit of a nuisance to women. There was trouble among themselves quite often. But that was just a few, most were good lads. I was the only regular policeman up by the barracks, the others were just war service men. I had to deal with all the complaints that occurred at the barracks. Later we had some English soldiers of the Royal Army Education Corps but there was no trouble. They were a different type of men, more the student type.

When the war finished in 1945 I did eighteen months beyond my retirement age. I was on the telephone in the station till I was fully retired. The police had their centenary celebrations in 1957 and with the other pensioners I was on parade for the last time. My first parade was in 1919 and my last in 1957.

JACK THOMAS

Postman

Jack Thomas was born in St Minver in the days when a postman's lot was very different from what it is today. Life wasn't easy, but Jack was a contented man.

My father was a postman who used to deliver the post, riding his bike in all winds and weathers around Pentire and Pentireglaze. He worked till he was over seventy. I went to school in Tredrizzick and when I left I went to work for a baker in Wadebridge, delivering bread and cakes by van to St Merryn, Constantine and Padstow and all around that area. After that I went to work for a grocer at Polzeath. I started as a postman at Polzeath. I well remember pushing the wheelbarrow of Christmas parcels up the steep hill there – that was before the post office used delivery vans, and I was doing a part-time round. After a while I put in for a transfer to St Minver and there I stayed until I retired, after almost forty years in the same village.

The mails came out from Wadebridge and I had to re-sort them. They included post for St Minver village, Trevanger village, Tredrizzick, Pityme and right down to Splatt in Rock, then over Trewint Hill and back to meet the main road again at Pityme. It would have taken some hours to walk it; that's why I had my post office bike. I've gone through several bikes. I wish I'd kept a record of the miles I've done – it must be thousands. When I retired I bought my old bike from the post office.

People sometimes ask me about dogs. I remember one summer there were visitors staying at the back of the bungalow beside the Clock Garage, before the present owner had it. There were two ladies in the garden sitting out in deck chairs. Two dogs nipped out of the garden and got me on the back of the leg. The ladies seemed to be asleep but they woke up and were surprised. They asked me if the dogs had bitten me. I told them they had. I think they must have been nurses, for they dressed my leg. Of course I had to report it. The police visited them and they were told they must in future keep the dogs under control. Another time I was bitten was up at Trewint farm. That dog got me in the back of the leg and I had to go down to the doctor to have a tetanus injection. For weeks and weeks the dog hadn't bothered me; he couldn't have been in a good mood that day.

Some days when I was out on my round, Mrs Ritter, the post mistress, whom I worked for, needed someone to deliver a telegram. When I came back she'd ask me if I could take it. I got paid extra for delivering telegrams. You see, mine wasn't an established round. I was just an auxiliary. My father's round was never established either. It was always auxiliary, not like the postmen in the towns.

At one time the post office at St Minver was down near the church. Mr and Mrs Cahart ran it. My father worked there before he stopped and I, myself, was there for a time. In those days there were three of us delivering. Parcels in those days, too, would come to the village post office for redistribution whereas now, for my round, they are delivered direct from Wadebridge. When Mr Carhart finished his letter round in the morning there might be six bags of parcels waiting for delivery. By then he had a van, so in the afternoon, when we'd had our dinner, we'd go round with the van and deliver the parcels. In almost forty years I've never been on the sick list – not one day in almost forty years, and I've had to deliver in all kinds of weather. When we had the last heavy fall of snow, I couldn't take the bike. You just couldn't move it. At last they got mail out from Wadebridge in a Landrover. I managed to deliver some on the main road but I had to wait till the next day to get the rest done on the hill.

I've had some interesting times as the village postman. One was with Prince Charles. He's a good lad. He paid a visit to the Duchy and came to the St Enodoc golf course. In the morning he went down to the golf club. Some girls were helping at the table. Prince Charles went into a room where the girls were and asked them what they were doing. They told him they had been sent in there, so he said he would stay and have a drink with them. He wasn't worried about the top people. In

44

the afternoon he came up to Westerly Boats. The schoolchildren were there and I had to go along with the mail. I was wearing my postman's gear. There were a lot of people there. A big policeman from Wadebrige told me Prince Charles would be delighted to have a word with me. Well, Prince Charles was coming down the line and he came up to me and said, 'I see you're a postman,' and he laughed and said, 'What have you got there?' On an impulse I took off my old postman's cap and put it on his head. He was delighted. We all laughed and he had his photograph taken and everybody including his two detectives took it in good part. I had mail in my hand and he remarked that the post would be late. Somebody told him, 'He's the singing postman'.

We talked for a few minutes and I told him I had once applied for a job at Buckingham Palace in the stores for the kitchens and he asked how I got on.

'Well, they told me that after consideration, they thought I'd be better off in sunny Cornwall.' I replied. 'I think so, too,' he said.

Later I sent the photograph up to Prince Charles at Buckingham Palace and I got a reply from his secretary that Prince Charles thanked me for the photograph and had happy memories of his visit to Cornwall.

It's not just the postal services that have changed. There's a different spirit in the people. Hundreds of what we call foreigners have taken holiday houses here in Cornwall. Some can be a bit standoffish, you know, a bit snobbish; some, not all. I once spoke to an army-type man in a café in Wadebridge. We had been speaking about Mrs Simpson and Edward, Prince of Wales. He said, referring to people like Mrs Simpson from abroad, that we didn't want their kinds over here. I told him, 'Look, when we depart from this life, if there's such a thing as a life after, and if we get to the other side, we'll be all on the same footing. There'll be no differences or class distinction there. We'll all be on the same level.'

There's a real spirit of friendship among Cornish people. When I go down west, say to Camborne; I know a lot of men in the choir down there; they always remember me and if they can't recall my name, they say ''Ow be, pard?' If I visit old haunts they still treat me as if I had only gone last week. But

45

there's not the same mixing now as there used to be with people coming in from other parts. Some folk, for instance, who come for the sailing at Rock seem to think they're in a class of their own. St Minver's not the same either. So many of the old people are gone. A lot of people from outside Cornwall come and buy up places, then they sell them, make a bit of money and move on. They don't settle.

We used to have all sorts of social activities run by the Cornish. We had Conservative dances down in the Pavilion. Mr Mobley who had the bus services used to run them. I played with Mrs Singer's band in Wadebridge. Mr Harper formed a band and I played with him over at Atlantic House. We had lovely times.

I've always played the accordion by ear. I travelled all over with Mrs Singer's band. She was a pedlar before she got married. Her father used to play the violin and her daughter used to sing. In the days before discos, we did two or three dances a week. We'd go down as far as Hayle on a Saturday night and up to Devon. We had so many jobs we had to split the band.

There are many people throughout Cornwall interested in music who know me. I'm a member of the Wadebridge Male Voice Choir. I was also a member of the well-known Treviscoe Male Voice Choir for several years and of course I played my accordion, as I said, in different dance bands. I took part in the Carol Levis Discovery Programme once, and I've had a lot of pleasure entertaining the inmates of old people's homes. I started with a small accordion that I bought for a few pounds. The one I've got now would cost hundreds of pounds but I got it with a trade-in for £15.

The postman is everybody's friend. He's kind of special with the public. I think what the children of Tredrizzick school did for me when I retired shows this. They presented me with a jumbo-sized envelope addressed to *The Best Postman in the World*, and marked *Special Delivery*. Inside there were two illustrated books, one compiled by the infants of four and five years old and the other by the older pupils. They touched on aspects of my career – a picture of me delivering the mail, singing as I rode my bike; me playing my accordion; struggling through the rain and snow; arriving at school with the post, and the dogs

9 Walter Boyd in his operations room

10 Walter on the helipad at Sennen

11   The old Bodmin police station where Frank Pooley trained

12   Cornish Constabulary, 1936. P.C. Pooley front row, 2nd from right

13   A presentation to Jack Thomas by local schoolchildren on his retirement

14   The former post office at St Minver

15 Jack with staff at the Trelawney Nursing Home

16 Miss Elizabeth McGuigan

17 Mr Victor Richards at the old Port Isaac school

18 Elizabeth McGuigan (bareheaded) with staff and pupils at Lanhydrock school

19 Respryn Bridge

20   Agnes Burgess, aged 16

21   Agnes's parents at their cottage door

22 Eric Worden, on right, in cap

23 Eric Worden, engine driver

24   Gang No. 37; Tom Dyer at left in braces

25   Gang No. 37; prizewinners in track maintenance

which did not appreciate the postie as much as the children did. Their wish for me was a long and happy retirement. They also gave me a two-pound tin of biscuits. These were among many tributes I received – marks of the affection that existed between me and many of the people I got to know on my rounds. The inmates of Trelawney Nursing Home presented me with a quartz clock in appreciation of what I'd done for them and for the entertainment they'd enjoyed when I played my 666 accordion for them. Mr Stafford, a post office official, came up from Truro and I told him about this and he said that people don't say a lot but it showed how they've appreciated what I'd done for them.

People used to tell me they heard me coming down to Tredrizzick in the mornings singing. I've made many friends through my singing and playing. I still visit the old folk in Trelawney Nursing Home. The owner says, I'll always be welcome there. I've always felt part of the people I've lived and worked among.

VICTOR RICHARDS AND ELIZABETH MCGUIGAN

Schoolteachers

VICTOR RICHARDS

I was a schoolmaster at Port Isaac from 1934 till 1962. My own schoolmaster must have thought I had some brains for it was he who encouraged me to go on with my studies. Although I was born and bred a Cornishman I went to learn the job of teaching at Westminster College, London.

In those days it wasn't easy to get a job. I finally got one in Walsall not far from the Grand Union canal. I'll never forget those early days. Every Tuesday three hundred pupils had to be deloused and even the teachers had to strip off in the classroom to be deloused too. It is no exaggeration to say that some of the pupils' heads seemed to be moving with lice.

The reason for this was the proximity of the school to the Grand Union canal. The children who brought vermin into the school were the sons and daughters of the bargees who sailed up and down the canal and had their families with them. When they tied up their barges the school's attendance officer would collect the children and take them off to school for the few days the barges were moored in Walsall before going on with their journey.

I wanted to get back to my native Cornwall. I got one teaching post, at Albion Road Boys' School, Torpoint, and then moved to Landulph before applying for a job at Port Isaac. Three candidates for the post were taken out for interview by bus from Wadebridge. I don't know whether the smell of fish put the other two off, but I got the job together with the old schoolhouse, which was in a dreadful condition and gave my wife and myself not a few headaches.

In the 1930s Port Isaac had a settled pattern of life. During the summer men and teenage boys went off on the yachts of the rich and turned their skilled seamanship into good money, for the lads had been brought up to handle small boats almost from the time they started school. Others worked inshore at crab and lobster fishing. In the winter most of the men fished the herring shoals.

This presented me and the school with a problem which might seem funny to most people but wasn't funny to me when I first started, although I got used to it. In the dim light of a winter morning the herring fleet would return with its catch. Small boats with older pupils from the school would row out to help deal with the catch and transfer it into the small boats to be rowed back to harbour.

While Scots lasses started to clean and gut the fish, the boys would come up to start school in thigh boots liberally bespattered with fish scales. The smell of herring was everywhere; it was not an ideal environment for teaching but it was all part of the boys' integration into the real working life of their village.

I wouldn't say life was easy in those days. The old schoolhouse needed plenty of work put into it and my salary to keep a wife and young family was £160 a year. But looking back I think the most important thing was that we were giving something that was vital to the lives of the young in the village and surrounding area. I have always believed in putting the pupils' interests before everything else. In those days things like strikes and refusing to do certain duties would never have entered our heads, even on a salary of £160 a year.

I have always believed in the parable of the talents. No matter who they are, every boy and girl has something in them that is worth developing. I remember one boy who, as we used to say, 'did not know the way out of the wet'; he wasn't very good at the three Rs. But unpromising pupil as he seemed to be, he had one great passion – the sea. He asked me if I could do something about getting him aboard a yacht during the summer. As a seaman he became a natural. On board one of the yachts owned by the Whitbread family he would climb up-top like a cat while the ship was pitching in heavy seas. Eventually he went on to become skipper of the Whitbread yachts. When Prince Philip wanted sailing instruction, my seemingly unpromising pupil from Port Isaac took him out on the Solent and thus he became a teacher of seamanship. It is interesting that the lad 'who did not know his way out of the wet' eventually went to Saville Row in London for the best yachting clothes money could buy. This lad is just one of many who prove that youngsters have something inside them and it's the teacher's job to look for it and encourage it.

I've had many really clever boys in my village school. It is when clever ones need to be stretched that one's own training and scholarship count. One of my lads finished up in charge of atomic research. Another became a barrister, another a doctor. Several received diplomas in mining at Camborne and went off to work in the gold mines of South Africa. In the nineteen-thirties there were grammar school scholarships awarded and when I was head at Port Isaac 132 pupils went on to the grammar school at Camelford.

Eight scholarships were awarded annually to schools in the Bodmin and District area. One year seven pupils from Port Isaac won them. That was a great year for the village.

Somebody asked me what my philosophy of education is and I've got strong views on that in the light of what I see going on in education today. At the age of eighty-five, and after fifty years of teaching children, I think men and women who have opted to be in the profession of teaching should take a good look at themselves and say 'What image am I passing on to the youngsters? If I'm putting my personal interests before their education, I'm not teaching them, I'm confusing them.' The tragedy today is that, although there are many good teachers, there are also those who by example are teaching children that the way to get more money for themselves is to withdraw part or all of their responsibilities. That's the road to diminishing public respect for what should be a great profession.

ELIZABETH MCGUIGAN

I spent all my teaching life in the little two-room school on Lanhydrock Estate, once owned by the Robartes family (headed by the Viscounts Clifden) but handed over to the National Trust when Viscount Gerald Clifden died. The school was about three miles from Bodmin and nestled in the lovely valley of the Fowey quite near the river. I lived and worked in

50

those beautiful surroundings from 1925 till 1961.

I came as a History graduate at the age of twenty-one and although I was offered promotion several times, I decided to devote myself to the children of the area. I well remember after I had been there for a few years one day walking through the woods in Lanhydrock. It was a beautiful day and the sun was sending shafts of light through the branches of the trees. A great sense of peace came into my heart and I knew this was where I wanted to be and I wanted to pass on this feeling of happiness to the children. I was in the right place and I knew it was for good.

I had to think out what being a teacher meant. I had to realise the child with two talents was as important to the teacher as the child with five. My job was to liberate the talents that were there so that the boy or girl could have a fuller and happier life.

The other thing was the realisation that Lanhydrock was a perfect nature reserve that offered great opportunities for learning many different aspects of life. It was on our doorstep and I had to make full use of it. With my first pay I bought a book on nature which became an environmental Bible for the school.

Over the years I had many examples of these two truths. For instance, one day, a boy who had glanced out of the window turned excitedly and told me there were about a dozen long-tail tits in the trees. I realised this was a sight one might never see again. I told them to take their bird-books, which were always available, and their exercise books and pencils, and that everything must be done with absolute quiet and without jerky sudden movements or the birds would fly off. First I had them open their books at the right page, then I said a few words, and keeping our fingers crossed we crept out behind the bushes. We were very lucky. I was able to give them a lesson, the quietest I'd ever given. The birds just sat there. The children never jerked their books or made sudden movements. We had a lovely lesson on that.

Another day an inspector was visiting the school when in rushed a boy from the playground with a wounded bullfinch. I made it comfortable in a little box and as it was a good opportunity I gave a lesson on the bullfinch both to the class and the inspector. He said afterwards he had thoroughly enjoyed his visit to Lanhydrock.

Sometimes pupils can do something you can't and that can give you an opportunity too. On one occasion I heard the sound of a tune coming from the playground. When I went out I found two of the boys playing mouth-organs in perfect harmony. I arranged for a jumble sale and with some of the money I bought six lovely Hohner harmonicas. I got the two boys to teach some of the other children and soon we had a school harmonica band to add to the percussion band and I got great pleasure in conducting it. The harmonica band played descants and the day after a television song contest they played the winning tune. When during the last war Princess Chula came to the school, the band entertained her. One pupil who had a tiny harmonica one inch long had to have a cord attached to it to prevent him swallowing it.

It gave us all great pleasure when we had our scholastic successes. Two of our pupils, Ronald Courtney and John May, came first and second in the county examination for special places when 2,239 from all Cornwall sat the exam.

Everyone at Lanhydrock was proud of the boys and letters of congratulation came to them from all over the county. Many of our pupils went on to Bodmin Grammar School. Some took degrees in London, became teachers or went into industry. One was a department head in Courtaulds. Another became a county councillor. He made an impromptu speech on behalf of Cornwall at a Regional Development Conference in Bristol which impressed Mr Callaghan, the then Prime Minister, and Mr Peter Shore who was the Minister for the Environment at that time. I always stressed that initiative was something the boys and girls should aim for.

I'm distressed at what is happening in education today. I don't believe in strikes. Doctors don't strike. They are committed to a principle underlying the Hippocratic oath. They are responsible for the bodily welfare of the human being. Teachers are concerned with the mental development of children. In strikes money is involved and that's directly between employer and employee. In a strike by teachers it is the child who stands in the middle between employer and employee. It is the child who suffers. In the case of pupils taking

'O' levels or 'A' levels or other exams they have worked for five or six years towards this goal, solidly and hard. To be neglected in the slightest way may put their success in jeopardy and affect the rest of their lives. It is a heavy responsibility. The simple sad truth is that as a whole – but with many shining exceptions – the modern teaching profession has edged away from idealism towards materialism. Looking back on the long happy years at Lanhydrock I have no regrets. We knew what we stood for.

AGNES BURGESS

A Cornish Childhood

I was born in 1908 in a little house with two rooms up, two down, near Respryn at Lanhydrock near Bodmin. It looked as if it had been dropped from the sky between woods and fields. Our landlord was the late Lord Robartes of Lanhydrock House and what a good landlord he was.

I can still smell the bread and cake taken from our oven and the pasties cooked under the baker in our oven fire-place. My parents, Kate and John Brokenshire, paid one shilling and sixpence a week rent. Later when we had the orchard added, I think it was raised to three shillings. I used to go to Sunday-school at the Gatehouse of Lanhydrock House owned by Viscount Clifden. I was fascinated by the circular stairway. Our Sunday-school sports were held in the grounds and if it was wet we went into the Long Room. After Sunday-school we went on to the little church in Lanhydrock estate. Our seats were behind the entrance door. The gentry entered by their own door at the top of the steps from their living quarters.

I remember the pans of milk with lovely crusted cream over the top in the dairy at Lanhydrock House. We would look down on them through the windows from the footpath to the church. It always looked so tempting. My mother did sewing for Lady Clifden. She was given a bulk of material to cut out and make up into dresses which Lady Clifden gave away to large families on the estate. I sometimes went up to the big house with Mother and we would be shown into Lady Clifden's own little sitting room, a small room and, as I remember, full of objects. I would be given a little low stool to sit on while they talked. The Clifdens were a wonderful family and very caring towards their tenants. When they had been out shooting my Dad would open the wood door to the path through our front garden. A pheasant would be handed to him and perhaps some kind remark would be made about his garden; that would make his day.

54

It was a sad day when the Hon. Tommy Robartes, Viscount Clifden's eldest son, was killed in the First World War. He was a fine fellow. My dad used to love to have a chat with him. He was a very friendly man and humble. We too had our losses when our only brother drowned at eighteen and a half. He was the only casualty through a collision just off Plymouth when he was on his way home for Christmas. As we were six girls and he the only boy, he was the pride and joy of my parents. Life was never quite so carefree afterwards.

I used to love to linger on Respryn bridge particularly when the artists were there, putting the beauty of it all on canvas. Lanhydrock drive was a favourite walk of mine, beautiful in those days, with azaleas of all shades, rhododendrons a blaze of colour and very well kept. Cyclists were prohibited from the drive after an incident when the carriage horses were frightened by cyclists coming round the corner. They bolted with the gentry inside while on their way to or from Bodmin Road station. I don't like to see the drive now. It's so different; I prefer to remember it as it was. Alas, memory is all I have of our cottage; it has been demolished completely. But I still have an oil painting I did, which I hastily finished before memory faded. Is there anywhere more beautiful than Lanhydrock? I am so glad it is well kept up by the National Trust. That walk up the avenue of trees seems to me as near perfect as anything could be. I rarely see it now but I can still picture the house full of servants and the grand family of Robartes still in residence.

There were two rooms in our little school at Lanhydrock, one the full length of the building and one smaller room with a little cloakroom adjoining it for the infants, with one lady teacher for each room. The one in our room took all subjects for all ages from infants to X7 standard, the highest class. Our day at school started with a scripture lesson and we were pleased and proud when members of the Robartes family came to hear us say the Commandments or Catechism. The Hon. Violet Robartes was a particular favourite of mine. She was very sweet and often came with Viscount Clifden, and Lady Clifden. The vicar also called in at school.

Reading, writing and arithmetic were of course among our main subjects; sewing also for the girls, our teacher being very particular over the gathers that had to be stroked down with the needle, and the scallops for our underwear which we made at school. These had to be marked out round a penny or half-penny, embroidered and then cut out.

During the war we made things for the soldiers; socks, where great care had to be taken in the turning of their heels, pyjama ties, and many other things. We also collected eggs for them. I was proud to get a certificate for collecting the highest number of eggs – 364 I think it was. I used to go to a farm on my way to school and Mrs Veitch would give me some eggs to add to our own hens' efforts. When we heard the sound of marching feet we would run to the edge of our playground to wave to the soldiers from Bodmin barracks on a route march. I can still hear the troops singing at Bodmin Road station, some so young; some, alas, never to return.

Empire Day was kept up at our school. The Union Jack would be hoisted in the playground, and we all marched single file around the flag and saluted, chanting our Empire verses.

Our Empire stretches far and wide across the deep blue sea
And in those unknown distant lands the Union Jack flies free.
Red, white and blue, these are the colours three,
The colours of our flag, another badge, you see
Red we wear for love, for king and country too
White for our young hearts, keen and brave and true
Blue we wear for hope, that's our Empire grand.

We would then play rounders in the field beside the school, the boys against the girls. We played with a racquet and a tennis ball then, not as they do today, kicking the ball. St George's Day we also kept as a special day. I remember we all received an orange from Viscount Clifden or Lord Robartes as we called him, and we had special games like cricket, rounders or hockey, all the equipment for the games being provided by the Robartes family.

Another thing I remember is the beautiful botany books we had. If we found a flower or plant we did not recognise we would ask to have the books down from the cupboard to find the name of it. They had beautifully coloured illustrations of all the wild flowers; each page covered with soft tissue paper to protect them. No wonder we grew up with a great love and respect for the Robartes family who provided them.

In the large schoolroom there was a fireplace at each end, one larger than the other. Around the fire was a guard and attached to the full length of the guard was a tray where we put our pasties to be warmed after playtime, when the monitor or pastie-girl would go out and turn them all until they got really heated through. In the summer I often took fruit pasties, perhaps gooseberry, apple or mixed fruits and Mother would give me a penny to go to the farm opposite the school to have a pennyworth of cream. Mrs Coad the farmer's wife would kindly cut a round off the top and put in a lovely dollop of cream. It tasted good.

One important event of our schooldays was the scripture examination and prize-giving for attendance. We had an examiner from away for our scripture exams and we all loved Mr Taylor, Daddy Taylor as we affectionately called him. We would go up Lanhydrock drive to meet him from Bodmin Road station. It was in the autumn and I remember we used to get chestnuts at the same time, opening the pods with our heels as they fell from the tree in the drive. I'm sure they tasted better than any we get at the shops today. When Mr Taylor arrived we would all dash towards him to see who could hold his hand on the way back to school. Scripture was my favourite lesson, nature study next and singing. The highlight of our school life was the prize-giving. Lord and Lady Robartes and other members of the family would come to present them to us – half a crown for each child who had attended regularly, one and six if you had only missed a day or two; packets of sweets for all the little ones. If you reached seven years' perfect attendance, as my sister Winifred did, among others, you were presented with a lovely little wristlet watch inscribed on the back 'From Lord Robartes for seven years' perfect attendance'. The boys would get a pocket watch.

We would walk up, each in turn, when our names were called, and with a little curtsy and a thank you, we would receive our prize from Lord Robartes. I am sure they enjoyed it as much as we did.

There was a rookery at the end of our garden, at the bottom of the school field, and if I heard the birds in full throttle, I knew I was late as they completely took over when the children went into school. Sickness kept me from school at times but I loved my days at Lanhydrock and shed tears on leaving, although I stayed an extra twelve months to make up for lost time. Our lady teacher, who stayed on after her retiring age, because of the war, was a marvel really. She was replaced by a new younger teacher from up-country. She was sweet and I enjoyed the little sketches we put on at Trebyan Institute. Lanhydrock was a little elementary school but what a wealth of happy memories it left me. There was never any violence. They were days of loyalty and caring, with a wonderful example set by Lord Robartes' family. And what a code set for us to live by – the Ten Commandments and religious training.

ERIC WORDEN, TOM DYER AND BILLY JOHNS
Railwaymen

The old Great Western Railway won the admiration and affection of thousands of travellers. Its trains, powered by those memorable steam engines the Star class, the Castles and Kings and later the Warship diesels, wound their way through farmland, past fishing ports and the tin and clay deposits to Penzance. The Great Western Railway was not just a gateway to a natural paradise; it had considerable economic impact on the crisscross patterns of trade and commerce within and to and from Cornwall.

Over the years, the railway workers of the Great Western faced many problems. One was the change-over, in 1892, from the broad gauge used in the Cornwall and South Devon lines. The tough feat of converting the gauge, with fifteen miles of obsolete displaced rolling stock lying in sidings, was carried out in forty-eight hours. Five thousand men toiled along the miles between Truro and Exeter laying the new gauge.

The name of Brunel is writ large on the railways of the south-west. But do you ever hear of the Eric Wordens, the Tom Dyers or the Billy Johnses, the ordinary folk of the Cornish railways?

ERIC WORDEN

I joined the Great Western Railway in 1936 at fourteen and a quarter. I was a telephone boy in the traffic department and I got fifteen shillings and fourpence a week. I answered all the telephone calls in the office at St Blazey. Calls would come in from all over Cornwall; Newquay, Par, St Austell and so on. Most of the messages in those days were coded. I remember the first message I received from Plymouth: *St Blazey to St Columb Rod – CABOB MEX AND B STADIUM DRAGON – Cattle wagon with vacuum brakes immediately required. Reply to this message.* This was different from the days when they used to telegraph by needles. After this job I took a fancy to steam engines. When I

59

was eighteen I was an engine cleaner at St Blazey depot. Just gone nineteen I became a fireman and was sent to Andover in Hampshire. The senior man would get the depot nearest to his home. I got up to fifty-four shillings a week. I was about twelve months at Andover as a fireman. From Andover I'd fire engines down as far as Southampton and north as far as Cheltenham. It was quite hard work. It was single line most of the way and you had to drop off a dozen single line tablets on the way. These were metal discs or keys which connected electrically from one signal box to the next, and were a safety device to prevent more than one train at a time driving a stretch of single line. You were supposed to get a 140 mile allowance 'extra money', but we didn't get it because to Cheltenam and back was only 138 miles. Next I went to Reading. I asked for a transfer there because of the big engines and main line work. At Andover we dealt with nothing bigger than the 63 class, Bulldogs and tank engines. At Reading I got on the Kings class, *King John 1626*. I got *King George V* which is still in existence. I was also on the Castles. The biggest ones were the Kings. Below that were the Castles.

At Andover and Reading I did both passenger and freight. You'd go with any driver and there would be a lot of goods traffic from Reading to Swindon, Banbury, Bristol, London, so I was getting plenty of experience. I was about twelve months at Reading.

Then I came back home to Bodmin in 1943. I'd only worked on the main line till then and I'd never seen anything like the twists and turns going from Bodmin to Wadebridge and Boscarne. I passed as driver and did spare driving to start with. When the GWR was nationalised there was a vacancy for a driver at Wadebridge which was now Western Region. I got the job. Wadebridge had been Southern railway with Southern engines, so I had fifteen months at Wadebridge driving the old Southern engines that they had kept; T9s, Drummond tanks and West Country. I liked the West Country which were streamlined. They were capable of doing ninety miles an hour in places in North Cornwall, going from Wadebridge right up to the main line from Plymouth, which it joined at Meldon and then went on to Exeter. In places you could have done ninety miles an hour unofficially.

As fireman and driver I had some hair-raising experiences, especially during the war. I remember an aeroplane coming down right onto the track in front of us. That was near Andover. It was a Bristol Blenheim bomber which had taken off from Andover aerodrome on a training flight. It lost height and crashed in front of us on a double track. Using the vacuum brake to full effect, we just managed to stop before we reached it. On a goods train you heard the bang, bang, bang from behind, as the trucks bumped into each other when the brake came on. It could knock a guard from one end of the van to the other. You've got to chance that, but the goods guards knew their job; they wouldn't just stand up in cases like that; they'd always hold on to something.

Another time we left Southampton terminus with a train for Cheltenham. It was a troop train with about five coaches on and a baggage van behind. We pulled into Southampton Central to pick up more troops. There had been an air raid and as we moved along, suddenly out of the blue, a bomb hit the back of our train. It completely shattered the baggage van. None of the troops was hurt. All it did was to cut off the baggage van, which was completely blown up, with all the troops' gear lost.

In another raid on Southampton, there was a 63 Bulldog class engine which had just come off the turntable as the raid began. The engine suddenly started blowing off. Of course they didn't allow that when there was a raid because the escaping steam could have been seen by enemy bombers. The fireman ran out, clambered up the other side of the engine and put on the injector which pours cold water into the boiler to prevent the safety valve blowing off. As he returned, a bomb landed on the other side. He was shaken but got to the shelter where we were. The engine was a write-off. The boiler had been peppered with shrapnel. I remember towing it back to Swindon three weeks afterwards. What amazed me was that in the tyres of the big iron wheels there were pieces gouged out with shrapnel.

Certain trains stand out in your memory. One of these was a special train for schoolchildren, bringing children from Padstow, through Wadebridge and up into Bodmin and taking them back after school in the afternoon. After they built the big school at Wadebridge, that reduced the numbers but there were still two coach-loads.

On the GWR you were brought up with the idea of safety, for instance regarding speed and speed restrictions. Of course you were issued with a rule book. But common sense and past experience were important.

Accidents could be caused by all sorts of things. For example I've known the line near the coast covered by spring tides, and sometimes there are faults in the equipment, but the main cause of accidents is human error. Certainly there were defects in things like points, crossovers and so on, but in my experience mostly it was the driver or signalman or shunter who made a mistake. Maybe a signalman would pull the wrong points service – familiarity can breed contempt – maybe a shunter wouldn't look carefully to see if points were right over and would call a driver on. Most of the derailments were in shunting. I've known runaway trains too but the only accident involving loss of life was when we lost a driver at Bodmin who came up with an engine from Wadebridge and collided with a goods train at Bodmin Road. I personally believed the signal was frozen – it was December – but they couldn't prove it. In passenger services, the GWR had a fine record.

I think a driver's biggest difficulty is night travel. It's absolutely necessary to have what we call knowledge of the road; you must know your track. You must know the sounds, the gradients, the bridges. You've got to have a photographic memory of it, especially when it's pitch dark. Here's an example: I left Exeter with a diesel and had fog the whole way except on Moorswater Viaduct, which was about 130 feet high, and was above the fog. That was the only clear piece of land I had from Exeter to St Blazey. In those circumstances you don't reduce speed. If you get the distance bells, electrically operated signal indicating that the section of line is clear, you know you're OK. But you had to know where you were, especially with a goods train which was more difficult to drive than a passenger train.

In those days, when you were going down an incline with a goods train, you had to let it run through or pull it through at constant speed because you might not have a continuous brake. You might have a couple of loose wagons behind. You mustn't get down to the bottom of an incline and then open up. You must keep going as smooth as you can with a continuous tight chain. With a passenger train you could slow going down and then increase power going up. With the wagons you had to go smoothly.

Of course this was the case in the old days, not now. All the passenger coaches have oil brakes and complete vacuum throughout. Before, in goods trains, you might have had four vacuums in front to assist with the braking but you might have had forty wagons behind, with just loose couplings. Driving a goods train in those days, you had to keep your wits about you.

We had to have a medical every five years and every twelve months or so for eyesight. We paid into a pension fund so we could retire at sixty. When you went to Swindon, as soon as you passed the medical, you paid five shillings to join the pension scheme, the Great Western Mutual Association. If you said you didn't want to belong to the scheme they told you they didn't want you on the job.

There's a lot of trouble now about the position of guards. In my day with the steam engines there was a guard, a driver and a fireman on a non-vacuum train. All three men were essential. The driver was driving it; the fireman was getting the steam; the guard was at the back looking after everything. If there was a fire, he could apply his brake and assist the driver. He wasn't in touch with the driver but from experience he'd know what to do. If he was at the top of an incline, he'd put his brake on and assist the driver. When he got to the bottom he'd take his brake off again. On all the slow goods trains he'd do the shunting at every station. But as time went on a lot of this slow work at different stations was done away with and fully vacuum trains came in with a continuous vacuum brake throughout the train which was operated not by the guard but by the driver. What happened when the diesels came was that the man who went out was the second man, the fireman. The guard came at the back of the diesel run and had a box wagon behind him and could see nothing.

There's another development coming which reduces the usefulness of guards. In many areas – I don't know whether this applies to Cornwall – if a driver gets into difficulty, he can get into touch with a signalman within a quarter of a mile of where he stops. He can plug in his phone every half a mile, into the cables along the railroad and ask for assistance. The point is that with this kind of communication the role of the guard gets less important.

Also more safety devices are coming in all the time. For instance, on most diesels you have the 'deadmans', a plate you put your feet on while you're driving. If you take your feet off the plate, immediately the brake goes on. A second safety device on the high-speed trains is a time-delay operation, where you get an automatic buzzer which tells you to press a pedal and if you don't do it, then the train comes to a standstill. You can't recover and then step on it to make the train pick up speed. You've got to reset and go on from stop. When you're travelling you get the buzzer every fifty-seven seconds or so, when you immediately press the pedal so the train keeps going. If you don't, it stops. It's a safety device that could prevent an accident with a runaway train. A guard would have no connection with this.

I was once on a runaway and I didn't feel too good! It illustrates the need for efficient maintenance on the railways. I had gone to Exeter with a 800 diesel, a Warship class diesel. The engine had been on between St Blazey and Fowey for three days. Now on that trip there was complete vacuum all the way through, so that you weren't relying on the brakes of the engine itself. I got this engine to take a train to Exeter. That was all right. But I came back light to Plymouth to drop the engine there where it was due for a service, and pick up another one. I came back to Plymouth engine only. Running light I realised the brakes were rather poor. I didn't think how poor they were till I came to the top of Hemerdon Bank. That's the incline going into Plymouth. When I went over the top to descend this bank, I realised I had a very poor brake and the further I went down the bank the faster we were going. We touched seventy miles an hour before we got down to the bottom. Luckily the brakes were working a little, but I could do nothing to stop the train. I had visions of another train down at the bottom waiting on a signal . . . I would have had no chance. Luckily when I got on the flat I managed to get it stopped. The difficulty had been that this engine had not been relying on its own brakes going to Exeter but on the train's vacuum brakes. I didn't realise until I drove the light engine back to Plymouth that it had such poor brakes. In later years, because they knew the diesels were coming, the maintenance on the old steam engines was bad. They let them run down until they were absolutely forced to do something to them.

Swindon in those days was a real railway town with the GWR owning the houses where railwaymen lived. If the men lost their jobs, they lost their house, they lost everything. If you were an ordinary labourer, say, you'd live in Bedford Street in a two-bedroom terraced house. But if you became a foreman, you'd go to a bigger house. The Great Western were good employers and they looked after their men and the men used to look after the Great Western. In a way it was something like the old tied cottages that nearly all farm labourers lived in.

I think before my time the old engine drivers took a personal interest and pride in their engines. That was more likely when a driver had the same engine all the time. But as things went on, you didn't get the same engine. Depots used to have certain engines doing certain jobs and certain men on them. Woe betide the engine cleaner who hadn't done a good job on them! The maintenance on engines previous to that was top notch. If a Great Western engine broke down then it made headlines because it was so unusual. I remember one connecting rod breaking at St Austell. The engine, a Hall class, was towed to St Blazey and all the side rods and connecting rods were taken off and sent to Swindon. They were very strict. You might have piston glands blowing or things like that but you didn't hear of an engine actually breaking down.

There were some real characters in those days on the GWR. Percy was one. He used to wear a trilby hat to his work. He wore it even when he was driving the engine. Percy was hauled over the coals several times because of this hat but he always came back with it on. It was all in fun but Percy boasted he was the best and biggest liar in St Blazey. He said he was more convincing than the others. One day the chief from Newton Abbot spoke to him: 'I've been wanting to see you. I'm not satisfied with the way the work is going on here'. It took the wind out of his sails when Percy promptly replied, 'Neither am I, Sir'.

Another Cornish character was Bill. He was a top notch

driver and had been at St Blazey all his life. He'd leave St Blazey with a goods train and he'd say to his fireman, 'The time is so-and-so; now you take this watch; we'll be passing Saltash at 18.54'. Then when they got to Saltash, he'd say, 'What's the time?' It would be spot on 18.54. That's the way to run a train, isn't it!

Ted was another one, with a great interest in mines. He was always prospecting for gold. He once showed me gold he had brought back from Scotland. When you think of all these men with all their different attitudes to life, we had a great variety on the GWR.

It's been a good life. In the 1930s you were lucky to get a job at all. I didn't like farming and I liked the railways, so there it was.

Today, Eric lives in active retirement in Lostwithiel, building without help, would you believe it, a family house for the future. Not content with that he rebuilds cars that have seen better days. His wife is in charge of the resources centre at Bodmin Comprehensive School. One daughter works on aircraft computers in Munich, Germany, the other daughter is a Doctor of Philosophy at Brighton Polytechnic.

TOM DYER

Tom Dyer lives with his wife in a house on the hill above Respryn bridge. It overlooks both the railway and the river Fowey. He was one of a breed of unobtrusive frontiersmen doing a humble job who deserve recognition in railway history. The safety of thousands of travellers on the old GWR was ensured by their work.

Walking up and down a railway track, day in day out for twenty years in all weathers, keeping it fit for trains to run on, you might think was not a very glamorous job, but it was a job necessary to the life-blood of Cornwall. That was Tom's job from the time he joined the railway, after five years in the Army, until he retired.

Tom, whose son also works as a shunter and cleaner on the railway, is as Cornish as they come, a stocky man with laughing eyes and a ready chuckle. He has a thick crop of grey hair topping a ruddy face that has weathered over years of rain, wind, sun, and snow. The house where he and his wife Ruby live looks down on the railway track to which he gave so many years of service.

66

It was marvellous getting a job right outside the door. I knew that bit of track like the back of my hand. Our hours were seven in the morning till five at night. There were six in our gang. The ganger, he was the boss. In the winter, and remember there was a lot of rain and sometimes flooding, we'd get our gear together in the morning. We had a piece of track marked out the night before that we'd want to raise and pack. We'd dig slack out until about breakfast time. Some places were very soft and wet if the country was hilly and the water would wash down. The track might sink and we'd have to pack it up; that's why we used to be called packers. Then we'd look at the rail joints to make sure they were properly plated up. The joints were always the weakest part of the rails which were maybe forty-five to sixty feet long. That was before the long welded rails of several hundred feet. The whole gang system is different now. There are mobile gangs who cover a longer stretch of railway. Each gang in my day had a certain length of track to look after. That's why the track maintenance men were also known as lengthmen in the old days – lengthmen and packers. We maintained the length of line from Respryn up towards Lostwithiel. We worked that length with pick and shovel and knew the whole of it. We had to, for many peoples' lives depended on it.

The ganger in charge of the gang carried his wallet. This might have the time sheets in it and all the details of the jobs to be done at a particular time. He'd walk from end to end of our length every day. Points had to be examined carefully. The ganger was the man responsible for the whole stretch. If the ganger was away I was acting ganger. My wage was about two pounds a week, with double time on Sunday and time and a half overtime on weekdays.

We had to get training for track maintenance. I went to school in Truro on Friday evenings. It wasn't an actual school building, just a waiting room on Truro station. Classes were held during the winter and one of the inspectors from the office took us. The other track men were the track layers. The laying always used to be done on Sundays, when there wasn't so much traffic on the move. Everything was got ready for an early start. There would be between forty and fifty men laying a piece of rail – everything was done manually. With all the lifting machinery nowadays about a dozen men will do the job. We could see the unemployment coming that we've got today.

I enjoyed my job. In my twenty years I was only called out on strike two days – two days in twenty years. There was a good spirit in those days. We were part of a railway community. The lads in the gang all lived around this part of the world, around Lostwithiel. You got to know them and you got to know the countryside beside the track. For instance, at one time, you'd see great salmon down in the river. You hardly see a fish now. When I've been working near Respryn bridge and then walking to Bodmin Road station, I've seen salmon hanging up on the posts in the division between the railway and the farmers' land – salmon nearly as long as the posts themselves. These were fish that had been rejected, because there was something wrong with them.

BILLY JOHNS

Billy Johns has retired after 35 years service on the railway. He started as a porter at Bodmin Road staton, now called Bodmin Parkway. He was in this quiet country station for the whole of his working life. Porter, booking clerk, senior railman, call him what you will, for regular passengers at Bodmin Road, Billy was as much part of the station as the booking office in and around which he served.

I started right from the bottom. At that time there was a station-master in charge at Bodmin Road. There were also two shunters, for there was a lot of goods traffic, whereas today there is none. There was also a porter-signalman, two leading railmen and three porters. I began as one of these. You can see that was quite a lot of staff for a small country station. Today the signal box is closed and all you've got is a booking clerk and two men on in each shift. That shows you how, as time goes on, with all the developments you need fewer men to run a modern railway. The grades are all changed too, to railman, leading railman, senior railman and so on. In the course of time they did away, as I said, with the station-master and I and another man were in charge at Bodmin Road.

In the old days there were two other stations in the area. These were in the town of Bodmin itself; Bodmin General and Bodmin North. My station, Bodmin Road, is three or four miles out from the town. The other two stations are out of use and we are the only one serving Bodmin. One big difference I've seen at Bodmin Road is the absence of goods traffic nowadays. It was once a thriving, busy little goods station with a goods shed and shunting going on all the time and a lot of stir about the place. Basic slag would come in on the trucks and be off-loaded into the goods shed. That went to the farmers to be put on their fields. There was also a big cement silo.

Cement wagons just like tanks would come in with powdered cement; they'd fit pipes down to the trucks and pump the cement up into the silo. Lorries took the cement wherever it was needed. China clay was also stored near the station. There was a lot going on connected with the farming community. For example we had cattle pens; boards were put down and the cattle and horses were driven up into the trucks; pigs as well. The farmers depended on the railway in those days. So there was plenty of life and noise about the place. I hope what has happened at Bodmin Road isn't repeated for goods freight all over Britain.

As time went on I saw the system of booking tickets changing too. The third class of the very early days disappeared. Remember those small cardboard tickets? You pushed one end into a date machine to have it stamped for the outward journey and had the other end dated for the return. Passengers handed over their outward portion to a collector at their destination. Nowadays the open station system does away with that and tickets are checked on the train. So many different kinds of concession fares have come in – for students, senior citizens, family tickets, weekend, monthly, three-monthly and so on – that even people working in the booking office might be forgiven for getting confused. Fortunately, British Rail are trying to simplify all this.

Another of the differences I've noticed over the years is the different attitude of railway workers. I'm not criticising folk but there seems to be a different spirit from the old GWR days. When a driver had his own engine for a period, he seemed to take an personal interest in it. Perhaps things were bound to

69

change when men were put on different engines. In the early days there was a really good friendly spirit. We pulled together. I did my job and enjoyed it.

I started on my first job at about £2 a week. One difference in wages between the station men and the track maintenance men was that they got double time on a Sunday and time and a half overtime during the week. We got time and three-quarters on a Sunday and time and a quarter during the week. Of course you've got to remember these track men were out in all kinds of weather and it was important to keep the trains running.

HOWARD MANKEE, B E M

Tin Miner

All his working life Howard Mankee spent underground in tin mining. After almost fifty years on the job he was awarded the BEM. Part of the citation reads, 'Mr Mankee started work at fifteen in Star Mines and joined South Crofty in 1936. He has worked in all facets of underground operations. Later he became shift boss in the mine and served as training officer for underground miners before being appointed as main captain. He is in the forefront of the labour relations scene and has earned the respect of men and management alike. Over the years he has taken part in many underground rescues. His alertness and conscientious manner in these difficult times have helped to save several lives. His knowledge of South Crofty's underground operations is unsurpassed by any other member of staff. He has great patience, understanding and loyalty and all who know him are inspired by his leadership and commonsense.' Howard is a founder member of the South Crofty Sports & Social Club. He used to play rugby and became a member of the Cornish Referee Society, serving as vice-chairman on the County panel.

Howard Mankee remembers the day when, as a lad, he went to the mine captain and asked for a job.

Mr Thomas was a big man. He had a little hut on Cooks Shaft which was his office. It was on the south side of the shaft so that he could see what was happening all round the shaft. 'What are you called?' 'Howard Mankee.' He said, 'That name doesn't ring a bell.' 'My stepfather works here – Reggie.' 'Oh, Reggie; does he know you are coming?' I said, 'No,' and I told him why I wanted to get into mining. He said, 'You can start on Monday but wait here till I get Reggie and see what he has to say.' My stepfather came up and said, 'I don't know what your mother will have to say.' But, as it turned out, Mother was quite happy and so I started working underground the following week.

I started as a machine man's mate or helper. In those days there was no training. You went into the mine and straight onto the job. The mine captain or the shift boss under him put you onto work with one of the men. The shift boss had a bit of the mine to look after and he would report to the mine captain and in turn the mine captain would report to the manager. That was the system.

I started work 'stoping' with a machine man called Jimmy Curtis. Stoping is mining the lode or vein of tin that is sandwiched between a hanging wall that is overhanging you where you're working and a foot wall. The lode or vein of tin is in between the hanging wall and the foot wall which carries the lode structure. There might be a width of lode only two feet wide, which would be difficult because there would hardly be room to work it. When I started three feet was a working width. A man could work in a stope three feet wide, but obviously it was different in a main drive where you had to get in trucks and equipment for the muckers to clear the debris. Nowadays locomotives and wagons are used for clearing.

The development ends of a drive were either six foot by six foot or on the manager's instructions, eight by eight. My job was to get the drills and with the help of the machine man to pull them by ropes up into the stopes. The machine man would plan the drilling and the firing. I would help to start the holes and hold the drill in position and when the hole was started I would get back out of the way till the next drill was required. Then I'd change the drills and put the next one up into the hole. In those days, whoever was operating the drill had to apply pressure to a handle to get it working. As you pushed you moved the cutting edge of the drill in an upward direction. The boy's job was also to pack the explosives into the stopes ready for the miner to fire when he was ready. Blasting was on a rotation system, for if a man was inside you had to wait till he came out. Then you'd fire and the man behind you would be waiting for you to come out and you'd tell him it was OK as you passed, so there would be no mix-up.

A natural event occurring 250 million years ago caused the eruption that was eventually to provide jobs for so many Cornishmen. At that time Cornwall and the Scillies were covered with sedimentary rocks. A terrific upheaval occurred which caused the granite to come up through the sedimentary rocks. There are six of these granite areas in Cornwall. One is at Hinkston Downs, a second at Bodmin Moor, a third at Hensbarrow. The next was Carnbrea around Camborne and Redruth, regarded at one time as the most mineralised zone in the old world, the Gwennap area having produced sixty-six different minerals. Carnmenellis was next and lastly St Just and the Land's End granites. The area around St Austell was a bit different from the others because the granite there had been altered and the felspar in it become china clay.

These six great granite blocks came up as molten material. As they cooled and hardened, cracks appeared and in the cracks were the materials which gave us tin and copper. Nearest the surface were lead and zinc; further down uranium, then copper, then tin, then wolfram. In the eighteen hundreds Cornwall produced three-quarters of the world's copper supply. There were 35,000 people employed in the Cornish mines at that time.

In South Crofty where I worked all the big mines were originally copper mines, and ten levels of copper down to about 1000 feet were completely worked out. There is a cavern down to that level and now the mining is in the tin zone below.

We went down through the first ten deposits of the old used copper deposits till we reached the tin. Tin lodes or seams or veins, generally speaking, run east and west, so you drive north or south and you hit a lode of tin. You work on the lode or seam and take out the tin like taking the jam out of a sandwich. In a good mine, the average amount of tin in that material is one per cent. You get roughly twenty pounds of tin for every ton of ore brought up.

One of the dangers is gases from explosives. We had at one time three chaps killed through being gassed. They went in the day after the blasting before the face was clear of the gases. Mine safety has been improved a lot since those days.

My next job after the stoping was in the development side, making main drives or tunnels. On the day shift the machine man and his helper broke up the material and on the night shift a mucker crew would come in and muck the stuff out and next day we'd come in and have a clear end. But in those days the drilling machine had the barn arm, a handle that had to be pushed, and the air pressure wasn't as good as it is today. It was hard work. We didn't have rotating bits and drills. And of course the muckers were also working by hand. No electric motors then, so it was a long tedious job. Two muckers shovelled into a wagon one working on each side. The wagons were emptied into skips which transferred the ore to the surface. From the top of the shaft it was transported over to the mill where it was crushed and broken up. The tin was separated from the ore by dropping to the bottom in water suspension tables. It finishes up as a powder which is sent off to the smelters.

At that time a machine man was getting nine guineas a month and for the nine guineas you had to do twenty feet of drive. For every foot over the twenty in a month, you got five shillings a foot. As a boy I got two shillings a day and after the first twenty feet I got an extra one shilling a day. I remember a machine man I worked with on the main development work, Herbert Mitchell. He was a homely, fatherly-like man who was kind to everybody. He was a great inspiration to us all. 'Now, son,' he'd say, 'do it like this,' or 'Now, son, hang on a minute,' and he'd show you. He didn't push us about, he encouraged us.

When war broke out I was called up. I was in the Territorials, and I was in the army till 1944. If you had any mining experience, you were taken out of the army and sent back to the mine. I came back to development work, to be a development miner, that is, pushing the main tunnels forward.

At that time they were experimenting with a new drill and I didn't realise at the time the effect my suggestions were to have. They tried out a new drilling machine which eliminated the old barn arm. They sent a demonstrator into the mine but no one seemed happy about it or was able to adapt to it. I worked alongside the demonstrator for a time and formed the opinion that the cylinder was inadequate to give the full thrust that was necessary. One day I was asked to use it, but I told them to take it back; it was no good, as there wasn't enough force of air in the leg to keep the machine rigid.

I made some other suggestions and the demonstrator went away. I thought no more about it until some months later when

74

they came back with another drill which had the modifications I had suggested to the demonstrator. At first nobody wanted to use it because they hadn't liked the first one. But when it was given to me to use I found it was a great improvement. Over the years more improvements took place. Today, that is the machine the miners use in the stopes, main drives and enters.

Over the years I got all-round experience in the mine. When we struck a rich lode I did the development, the main drive, the sub-development, the raises, the complete structure, which was about 120 feet long and 100 feet wide. By then I had done all the jobs it was necessary to do to become a miner.

At Cooks Shaft, a pump broke and we had flooding for a period of time. It was decided to put electric pumps in. Three of us were given the job of cutting a pump channel. They were Leslie Webster, a chap called Williams who had done some mining abroad, and myself. It took us weeks to get in because we were working in old workings that were very, very small and to get muckers in to help us it required height and width. Eventually we did it with the help of the fitters and engineers.

Once we had cut the pump station we went on from strength to strength. First we did the various drives for the pipes from the new pump coming back into the shaft, and then went down to 340 level where we cut another pump chamber for an electric pump. It was a real team job. The pumps are still working these chambers today. It was a job where all the operations came in – raising, stoping and development. We cut the water bays on the north side of the shaft so that we could pump the water into these bays as required. For me it was quite an experience.

All mining carries a certain amount of danger. I've been involved quite a bit in mine rescue. When I started there was only one first aider on the surface; that was Charlie Williams. He was responsible for dealing with serious accidents underground, but there was no organised first aid. In 1964 we started mine rescue and first aid teams. We had classes and the organisation grew and today we have one of the finest mine rescue and first aid teams around. We've had to deal with bad situations like folk being buried in stopes and in chutes. This is where teamwork is essential and knowing exactly what to do in an emergency. We were trained and examined by doctors. First aid training was voluntary but everybody did it after their work without any payment. Nowadays they have courses, lectures and day training and there's a doctor at the mine two or three days a week. Also there's a full-time first aid team in the mine throughout the twenty-four hours. Even when a first aid man is at lunch, he is still on call.

It has been interesting to see the changes in the labour force in tin mining in Cornwall over the years I've been working in it. It was traditionally a father and son industry with son following father down the mine, but things changed after the Second World War. First we had the Bevin boys during the war, then because the sons were getting jobs outside mining, they had to recruit Poles and then Italians.

I was made shift boss and the management decided that we would have to train our own men in mining so I was sent on an instructor's course at a training school in Hampshire, where I also took courses on safety. The management began to build up a training school which I was involved in. That was one reason I got the BEM award in 1982, as training officer for underground miners. So after all these years as a miner, I finished up as mine captain.

JACK YEO AND STAN YELLAND

Clay Workers

JACK YEO

Jack Yeo is no push-over. His stocky frame buttressed by massive shoulders and formidable muscled arms gives the impression of an irresistible tank. For forty-eight years he worked with china clay, from the days when muscle power was the great driving force, when men were lowered by ropes down the face of the clay and hacked at it with their dubbers.

Jack Yeo was born in the hamlet of Terras, in the clay country north of St Austell. His grandfather, who lived near Liskeard and came of farming stock, had a family of eighteen. Jack's father got a job in china clay and became the first of three generations of clay workers.

Here Jack gives a vivid account of his initiation into the industry.

I started as a kettle-boy in the crib-house. Nowadays you'd call it a canteen; that's where we ate. The men started at seven and broke at half-past nine for crib. The kettle-boy's job was to get the kettles on, make the tea and warm up the pasties. He was expected to go to the shop for papers, cigarettes or tobacco. He'd pick up the tools and take them to the blacksmith to be sharpened. You were green, just out of school and the men would pull your leg. They'd give you something to take to the blacksmith and say 'Tell 'im to sharpen both ends.' You felt a fool when you realised they were having you on.

I was fourteen when I left school and I was big and strong. The first thing I did was to go and see the captain; that's what the boss was called. Every boy had to see him first. Nine times out of ten there would be a job for you in the clay. He'd size you up and tell you to start with Tom or Dick or whoever.

The captain knew everybody and what they did. Well, as I

say, I was first a kettle-boy. Then the captain sent me to work at the kilns where the clay is dried and cut. I was there for two or three months keeping the pathways clean because you didn't want dirt to get in the clay. Then I helped the men tip the clay into wheelbarrows and it was loaded into trucks. The railway trucks would take it to the Potteries or to Fowey where it was shipped abroad. When I started I was getting eighteen shillings a week.

I went on to another job and this time I was put on a clay tip. You can see the tips from quite a distance, rising up like hills in this part of Cornwall. They put me up top, where I had to make sure that everything was in working order as the trolleys brought up sand which was one kind of china clay waste, for tipping. The waste consists of such things as the top layers of earth, sand and rock. I'd start from home at five in the morning for this job, going on my bike to the pit where I'd have a talk with my work mate. Then I'd walk up the slope of the tip, alongside the rails, right to the top. We had a little hut at the top where I could shelter when the weather was bad. We were on journey work, which meant we'd have a pitful of sand to be sent up and tipped, and when that lot was done we'd stop work. These big tips are caused by the dumping of the sand made of decomposed granite after the clay and mica have been washed out. Trolleys or skips took the sand up onto the tips, or burrows, as we called them. Now it is taken by conveyor belt. The top soil and rocks are moved by huge trucks that move more waste in a day than we could in months.

Another job I was put onto was moving the overburden, that is the mass of earth and rocks that cover the clay and must be removed before you can get at the clay. We did it all with our shovels. Later it was done with machines and dumpers. It was hard slogging, as there might be five feet or fifty feet of earth above the clay. The men were on piece-work; the faster they shifted it, the more money they got. We youngsters did as we were told. The men would load the earth into trams and we'd push them away. Later I got on to the loading.

In those days the men used to be lowered down the clay face held by a rope tied to their belts. A man would hammer at the clay with a dubber, a kind of pickaxe, but where a pickaxe has two prongs a dubber has one. There could be quite a drop below you; maybe fifty or up to a hundred feet. The rope was attached up above to a big iron bar in the ground. A bloke would fill the holes with dynamite and explode the face. My son is in the drilling now. Modern electric drills can go in fifty feet with no bother. We had to slave at it with hammers. The clay was washed out with hand-held hoses and the men worked in all kinds of weather. Now you have men in huts and a press of a button sets off the hoses with terrific pressure. The sand and clay and mica were all washed out into the sump and pumped up from the pit. In the old days it was big water wheels that drove the pumps.

I've been asked about accidents in the pits. Avoiding them was a matter of commonsense and we knew our jobs. The captain kept an eye on things. Nowadays they've got safety officers in works and factories. In our time if you thought a job was dangerous you could talk it over with the captain. He knew everybody and he knew what the men could do, but in the end you had to use your common sense. In forty-eight years as a clay worker I had one minor accident to a finger.

For a couple of years I went to work in the kilns where it was hot from the fires. I'd leave home at four in the morning at this time. I wore clogs with irons on them and if you were in the kiln shed for ten minutes, it was so hot on the feet you had to get outside and stand in a small stream. Your clogs would steam and that was just after ten to fifteen minutes inside. Sometimes the handle of your shovel got too hot to hold. But it wasn't always as bad as that.

There would be two or three coal fires to a drying pan. There were three men working in the kilns. We got £12 to £14 a week then. There were different levels of pay for different ways of working. Apart from the kettle-boys, the lowest worker was the 'underscount'. These were the men on journey work at a fixed rate, and there were also those on piece-work. I was lucky because I was never underscount. I was on piece-work a lot where you could work fast and make the money. I was big and strong and I could work hard.

I had to think of money when I got married. There was a time when I had to start from home at 3.30 in the morning and I'd come home and have a bit of lunch and sleep for about two hours. Then I'd go out to the haymaking for a neighbouring farmer. That brought in a bit of extra cash.

The industry has changed so much in recent years I hardly know it now. The way clay has always been extracted is by washing but the techniques have changed with the years. In the beginning hill-side sites were selected for excavation because a stream could be diverted to run down the face and wash out the clay which men had loosened by their picks or dubbers. It flowed down to a washing place where the diggers' heavy boots trampled on it till it resembled a pond of whitewash.

As time went on the excavations went deeper and they became pits from which pumps were needed to pump up the clay slurry from the bottom. The old hand-held hoses which washed out the clay were later replaced by giant hoses with pressure of 300 lbs. per square inch, operated by remote control.

The earlier catch-pits where first the coarse sand and then the mica settled were succeeded by the modern sand drag from which the clay slurry flowed on to the settling pits. Before it reached them, blue or pink dye was added to it to prevent discolouring. Water continuously ran through the settling pits and tanks before the clay, now pure, went to the kilns to be thoroughly dried and sent off to different destinations.

After years as a clay worker, I switched to another job in the same firm. I was foreman of a gang of men on construction work, building the foundations of different kinds of buildings in Cornwall and Devon, but still with the company, working with materials that came from clay.

We laid foundations. If these were wrong, everything else would be wrong so we had to be accurate. Before this I had been involved in making building blocks by hand – 18" x 9" x 6" made from sand and cement with chippings in them. The company also made breeze blocks from ashes. When I did this sort of work I started at seven o'clock and used to make up to 500 cement blocks a day by hand. Only the fittest men could do that job. We had a fellow mix the sand and cement and we'd do the rest – moulding and pressing. I was on piece-work. You had to work quickly but get them right. Nowadays a blocking machine will turn out 3,000 a minute.

In the early days each man had his own tools, his own shovel and dubber and so on that were provided by the company. Today workmen get working clothes too – boots, shoes, trousers, and overalls. We bought our own clothes except the man on the hose, who was provided with thigh boots.

I've been asked if I ever wanted to be a works captain; but I'm not one who wanted to be here today and gone tomorrow. There were fellows about my age who would ask to be moved to another job. I was content with whatever job I was doing and got on with it. I don't regret it. It was hard work, but, as I say, I was content.

Our company is a good one and looks after its pensioners. In 1984 they erected a huge marquee at their headquarters at St Austell and invited several hundred pensioners. We had the works choir entertain us and they laid on a dinner. Of course there's a pensioners' dinner every year, with food, drink and entertainment and each Christmas every pensioner gets a box, of about £12 to £15 value. The company does not forget its old workers.

I don't know what Cornwall would do without its china clay and all the thousands of jobs it provides. They reckon tourism is our most important industry but if the clay finished, I think it would be the finish of Cornwall.

Over the years there weren't just changes in the way clay was obtained, there were changes in what it was used for. At first it was for pottery and then porcelain. There's not so much of it used for that now. Most of it is used in paper-making. It's mixed with pulp for making good quality paper because it gives a glossy surface. But you find it now in plastics, in PVC and fibre glass, and floor tiles; it is used in the rubber industry and for making paints. It's even used in medicines and in leather and textiles, and fertilisers. It's getting difficult to think what it's not used for. I've not been able to keep up with all the changes in the china clay industry.

I have a great respect for the skill and craftsmanship of the clay worker. I've known blokes who could neither read nor write but you couldn't tell them anything about their job they didn't know. There was a carpenter who was both deaf and dumb – we had carpenters and blacksmiths working for the company. You just had to show him an object, a box or something you wanted, and he'd make a perfect job of it. He was a born craftsman who knew his work from A to Z. I did a

81

bit of striking for the blacksmith and he was the same. Nowadays carpenters' machines turn out a lot of the work, and the old breed of craftsman is dying.

When a man works at his job for forty or fifty years he knows what he's doing. I've never been to college like the young fellows who are coming in now, but experience must count for a lot, that and hard work. After I'd done a good day's work the boss would come and say 'You've done a damn good job; I'll put a quid in for you next week.' That kind of thing doesn't happen now.

Apart from the General Strike of 1926 I've not heard of a strike here. I certainly have never been involved in one. There have been strikes at the ports, I believe, on the transport side in modern times, but not in my time.

I was never one of those that thought of my work and nothing else. I certainly took a pride in my work and got some good reports, but when I was away from it I didn't think about it. There were some old fellows who went to the local and talked about nothing else, every night. They'd eat, sleep and drink work; they never got away from it. If I wanted a pint or two, I'd never go to a local pub. It was enough to hear about work when you went in next morning; then you put your mind to it.

After twenty-five years' service you got a gold tie-pin from the company: I also got a gold watch for forty-five years' service.

The end of my working life in the clay industry didn't mean the end of being involved in things. I think I put my leisure to good use. I am an active member of the Mid-Cornwall Group of the National Association for the Welfare of Children in Hospital (NAWCH). I am a firm believer that children in hospital, especially children under five, need their parents to be near them and that the ideal situation is unrestricted visiting and residential facilities. There should be a welcome for parents visiting hospitals. Trained teachers and playworkers should be available as play and education are important for children. Our Mid-Cornwall Support Group arranges transport for parents in emergencies to local hospitals. The group organises dances and jumble sales. My wife makes woollen goods, patchwork cushions and baby clothes for these sales and my daughter makes toys and dolls for the same purpose. My wife, until she retired, nursed mental patients at St Lawrence's Hospital in Bodmin.

STAN YELLAND

In the early 1900s Stan Yelland's grandfather was captain of a clay pit. His father also worked in clay. Stan in his turn became captain of Rock's pit in the Bugle area. He started as a kettle-boy in 1930 and worked in clay till he retired in 1980.

I was captain of Rock's pit at Bugle and before that I had been second captain. Everyone started under an older man who had more experience than he had. I was captain till I finished in 1980.

When I became captain of that pit, my main duty was to produce a target of clay per week. When I went to Rock's pit, it produced 800 tons a week; by the time I retired in 1980 we were producing 3,500 tons a week. It shows how the industry has progressed and clay was selling that much more all over the world.

We started at seven in the morning and the shift lasted till half-past three. I would get to the pit in good time to read the reports of the afternoon shift boss and night shift boss to see if there were any problems and if anything had gone wrong. If anything had broken down I had to get the engineers and electricians quickly on the job. There were men who had to be given certain jobs starting work at seven, and I had to make sure machines and equipment were at the right place. So I was very busy first thing in the morning.

Years ago the captain was the man in the pit. He hired and fired; it was his job to take on men and when it was absolutely necessary and not before, he sacked them. The captain always had a manager above him but years ago the manager would only come round, say, once a month, and we always knew when he was coming. Later a manager was put in a pit with you and he was there nearly all the time. It worked well in my case because I was a practical man, having started long before the war as a kettle-boy, and I knew all the jobs inside out. I went from kettle-boy right up through all the jobs in the pit until I became captain. In the early days the manager who had been above you came, nine times out of ten, from the Camborne School of Mines. He had the theory and the captain had the practical experience so if you got on all right with the manager and worked together, it was a lovely combination. But as time went on the captain's status started to fall. Years ago he was the leading man in the pit and had a company house with free rent and rates. But all the privileges started to die out when they brought in the young managers.

Safety was a very important factor for the captain especially with the Health and Safety Act coming in the later years. There was a greater chance of accident when machinery came in a big way – dumper trucks over the tip, bull-dozers upset, that kind of thing.

Of course the changes in the industry itself were tremendous with the passing of the years. I remember working up in the stopes. In the beginning we would be working eight or nine men in a row breaking into the clay with our picks or dubbers. Then they'd turn the water on what we'd broken up. After that we'd move over – breaking in the streak we called it – and break up a new stretch. Later we used jumpers, an iron bar sharpened at one end which you lifted up and then dropped on the clay, turning it as you dropped it. We'd maybe go down about six feet and put in a few sticks of dynamite and blast it. When the big hoses were introduced, the clay had to be blasted and broken up a bit. Now of course to produce their target of over 3,000 tons they've got rippers and bull-dozers. The manager sometimes asked me if we couldn't do away with the 'dozers for a few months, and I'd remind him that we couldn't reach our target without them. We needed machines because china clay is very hard; you couldn't get your target without machinery and blasting.

The role of captain in a clay pit called for a lot of qualities in a man. The first thing was to know what china clay was all about, and what you were producing. It wasn't a matter of getting out 3,500 tons of any grade of clay. You had standards of clay to aim at. This meant knowing what hoses to use as these were located at fixed parts of the pit where the grades of clay might be of different quality. You had to get the quality of clay the company could sell. You see we numbered our hoses or

84

monitors in the pit. Suppose I wanted grade B clay which is a fairly high grade, I'd tell them to work No. 1 hose for two hours one shift, then work No. 3, but leave out No. 4 because it wouldn't make grade B. The purpose of the monitors was to wash out the grade of clay you required.

The other quality a captain needs beside knowing about clay is an ability to handle men. Men would come to me with their personal problems, problems about their home life. Everything was absolutely confidential; they weren't just workers, they were my friends and they trusted me. The better I could serve them the better they worked for me. I had done all the jobs myself so I knew what a man could do in a day, and I spoke their language. In this job it was important to know how to handle your men. The army helped me in this for when war broke out I joined up. I rose to the rank of sergeant instructor and learned a lot about handling men. I wanted to be a captain in the industry and I had the feeling I would be all right in the job.

Before the war I had learned about the effect of chemicals on clay. At first the way we refined clay was to have a few runs, traps that took out the rough stuff and mica. Then chemicals started to come in. In 1937 they picked me out to become a chemist so I had to learn about refining and purifying. They tried to get me out of the army on early release, when the war was over, because they needed me at the clay works. When I did get out, I was sent, as I had been before the war, from pit to pit to teach two or three men about chemicals, and then they would take over that work. Then I saw I had a chance of becoming second captain and from there I became captain.

I've had a lovely life with the company; I'd never wish for anything better. One of my happy memories is the good fun I used to have with the men. I used to get to the pit at twenty to seven in the morning, so I had time to tell them what I'd been up to the night before and we'd tell each other what we planned to do that evening, what was on, one thing and another. It was a social time which put us all in a lovely mood. By five past seven the men were on the job and in a good humour. I looked after them in ways unknown to the bosses, and it paid off because I could get them to do anything for me. If I had been hard, they'd maybe have said 'Sorry you've got a break-down

85

but I'm playing darts tonight.' And that was one of my biggest headaches: if there was a break-down, I had to get things going again. Sometimes I'd go home at half-past three and be back again in the evening or again in the night to see how the work was getting on. And when I called on the men to help me out they never let me down.

When I was working I lived almost beside my work but I came to live in St Austell ten years ago. It's fine here, with two flat bowling greens near me and the county library just over the road, and a club nearby. Now I'm a works guide. We go anywhere under the company. If there's something new we'd like to see, the management let's us see it. I'm still very interested in the company after fifty happy years.

WILLIAM AND LOUISA CHELLEW

The Blacksmith and his Wife

The last of the St Minver blacksmiths is dead but his wife, Louisa, is a bright ninety-six year-old, living happily in a home for retired citizens overlooking farms and fields on the Camel estuary. Louisa tells their story.

Like most blacksmiths William Chellew, who came from a farming family, was a big, brawny man, one of whose great interests was Cornish wrestling. He loved watching Cornish wrestlers. He'd visit games where wrestling took place all over Cornwall. He'd wrestle with anybody just for fun. Another was bell-ringing; he was a great bell-ringer. I've got two silver medals that he won ringing with his team for St Endellion Church. He went to St Endellion twice a week, but on Sunday he went to St Minver. St Minver ringers weren't so keen on contests and William loved these, so he'd walk all the way to St Endellion twice a week, and that's quite a distance, about ten miles there and back. He was really enthusiastic. On Easter morning he'd get up at six o'clock and go round calling up the other bell-ringers. The same on Christmas morning and they'd ring, too, on New Year's Eve. He went all over Cornwall ringing.

William loved children and they all loved him. They would come and watch him at work and he'd play with them. He would get them in a field during their dinner hour and he'd teach them Cornish wrestling and he'd give them all a penny. A blacksmith's shop has a great attraction for children with the work going on – the hammering and the sparks. He kept his tools in splendid order. They would watch him doing soldering and mending the old box irons that women used in the old days and when he was soldering he would use borax powder. Blacksmiths seem to make many friends. They are important people in a farming area.

William knew all the farmers. They'd bring in their horses and he'd go out to repair their farm implements. Farmers in those days were poorer than they are today and they often found it difficult to pay their bills. There's so much money around today people don't seem to look after it and put the value on it we did. There was always mending going on in the homes and in the farms. We don't seem to mend much nowadays. We had a lot of bad debts when the farmers couldn't pay William. He was easy going and he would say, 'Well, if they haven't got the money, they can't pay.' I'd say, 'But you've got to pay your traveller, he's got to have money to pay his bills.' Yes, the farmers were poor. The bills weren't big at all, yet at times they hadn't the money to pay them.

That was one thing that struck me when I came to St Minver. It was a poor community. The houses were clean but there was no comfort in them at all; plain slate floors, one little tiny mat in front of the fire-place, bare kitchen table and chairs – that's all they had. They did their cooking in old-fashioned F. & J. Martyn coal stoves from Wadebridge. Most just had one room.

When William brought me home to St Minver, it was indeed a village with few facilities, as most Cornish villages were before World War One. We had no electricity and no main drainage. We had to go right down the hill by the church and across fields to fetch drinking water. My husband went to get it. He had a well near the blacksmith's shop which he used for his work but it wasn't drinking water. What happened if we wanted drinking water was this. If you went at nine o'clock, the squire would pump up water to a tap at the bottom of the hill. If you were late, you would have to go down the hill, over the stile and, as I said, across two fields. We had tanks behind the house for rain-water. I used that for cleaning and washing. We got lovely real clotted cream from the farmer when he came on his milkround, not like the stuff you buy today.

William's main work was horse shoeing and repairing farm implements but he also did a lot of wheel-binding. A friend used to make the cartwheels and he'd help William to put the iron bands on the rims. It was very heavy work with the big cartwheels. They used to bind the wheels on the millstone that stands in front of the Old Forge Garage. They'd lay the millstone flat on the ground beside the entrance to the shop and put the wheel on it, then bring out the red-hot band and hammer it over the wheel. William's friend, Mr Goodman, who was the village carpenter and wheelwright, kept pouring water on the rim to cool it and as it got cold it shrank onto the wheel.

There wasn't much William didn't know about horses. There were some quiet ones and some kickers. William had absolutely no fear of any of them. Some of the big cart-horses had feet like frying pans. I remember a gypsy once brought in a horse and asked him to shoe it. He said he was going to Rock and would pick the horse up on his way back. My husband began by stroking the horse but it was a kicker. It kicked and went on kicking for about half an hour and almost knocked the shed down. William at last took a stick and gave it a good thrash and the horse at once stood still. He never moved while William shoed him all the way round. When the gypsy came back to collect him, William said quietly, 'You didn't tell me he was a kicker'.

He handled some really difficult horses in his time. It wasn't easy, especially when horses leaned on him while he was shoeing them. He charged seven shillings and sixpence for shoeing a horse. He'd get the iron from Wadebridge and Plymouth. He made the big gate for St Minver House near the church for the squire, Mr Sanford. Of course it wasn't just horses William dealt with. Once he had to trim a bull's feet! The feet had grown so big that the vet came and asked him to do the cutting. He often worked with the vet on animals' feet and sometimes got kicked on the shin. The way a horse behaved with the blacksmith depended a lot on what had hapened the first time it was shod. If it had been hurt, the horse would never forget it.

When William was a farrier in the army during the war, he also had to shoe mules. Farriers didn't like that job. The mules were stubborn animals and took some handling. They were supposed to shoe one mule each before breakfast. William would go round with his torch in the dark and pick a mule that was sleeping and wouldn't be so active!

Once a farmer sent a boy with a horse that no one else could shoe. I'll never forget it. It was a big cart-horse. He had to get it into a field or it would have kicked the shed to pieces. He got help from a neighbour but the man and boy together couldn't hold it. After a bit they managed to get the horse into the shed and he finished the job. But he told the farmer afterwards, not to send that horse out again with only a boy in charge.

William gave much in effort and time to our small community. I tried to do my bit too. For thirty years I collected from farmers and villagers for the district nurse, Miss Shepherd, trudging on foot every spring and autumn to collect ten shillings from the farmers and five shillings from the cottagers. I had some skill in nursing and I served with St John's Ambulance, so people would seek me out if the district nurse was not at home.

We were all at one in the village in the old days. Everybody was so friendly and everybody would help everyone else. There was a girl who had been ill for a long time. Every Friday, I used to wash all her bedding because she lived alone. Then next door to me, I went in to help when a first baby was born and looked after the mother for a fortnight; I used to bath the baby every morning. I gave my neighbour's children a bath on Saturday nights. During the war I worked with the St John's Ambulance at the vicarage, with children evacuated from London. I did full-time nursing in the sick-bay, from nine till five. Although all my other work was voluntary, I got £1 a week from the council for my nursing. I spent one day a week at Polzeath making towel bandages for the troops. That was run by the WVS. I joined the WI when it was just five years old and I took part in every class, for baking, mat-making, lamp shades and so on. I won a bronze medal and certificate for cooking and making brown and white bread. I was in the WI for twenty-seven years. Every Saturday for thirty years I helped with the cricket teas. Cricket was a popular game in St Minver and Rock. There was great rivalry. I loved sewing and embroidery, and gardening. There was a lady at Tregenver who kept rabbits. She had the skins cured and cut out gloves which I made up. I would make four or five pairs of gloves and moccasins each week.

I've led a simple life, among friendly people. Everything we ate was good wholesome food. Nowadays it seems to come out of packets. I eat a lot of salads and cold meat. All the walking I did helped me too. Miss Shepherd our district nurse was also a great one for walking. She never had a bicycle, and walked everywhere. I suppose it's the ordinary things like being contented and having good food and a bit of exercise that's the secret of living. Looking back, it was a simple life we led; we made our own enjoyments like socials and public teas and concerts, when the squire would be chairman. I always liked singing and I belonged to St Minver Church choir for many years and also the WI choir. You know I can still sing at ninety-six and they're amazed at me here. With the choirs we sang all sorts of things but nowadays it's mainly hymns I sing. I think a person should keep her spirit up. I take a great interest in what's going on with my radio and television. Life is full of interest.

JACK BONEY

North Cornish Farmer

I was born at Copplestone farm in 1898. Copplestone near Boscastle, which my father farmed, belonged to an independent farmer, Dr Wade. When I was in France during the First World War, Dr Wade died and Copplestone came up for sale. It was sold for £2,850 which was more than my father could afford. Later my Uncle Tom bought it on behalf of my father.

When I returned from France after three years in the army, I went to work with my family in a rented farm, Tremorle, in St Tudy parish, where Thomas Hardy wrote the book *A Pair of Blue Eyes*. I did the hauling with horse and cart, and worked in the fields with my brothers. My mother died of cancer there in 1921. Just before she died, we got an ultimatum from the landlady who owned the farm to say we must pay the rent or move out. She had raised our rent as so many rents were raised just after the war. On her death-bed Mother told us to comply with the request, so we stayed on but we were losing money all the time. The man we employed to do the hedging was better off than we were. We lost £1,100 in fifteen years but the hired man was getting paid for his work. We decided things couldn't go on like that so we stopped renting Tremorle and returned to the farm at Copplestone where we could keep twice as much stock.

I decided to try to build up Copplestone. First I went to London and bought a lorry. I used it to go to the beach at Rock for 2,000 tons of sand, all loaded by shovel, to put on our fields. On Sundays I'd do three loads a day, which would take me three hours each time. It was thirty-three miles each way, almost 100 miles a day, using nine gallons of petrol at one shilling and five pence a gallon.

Then I thought to myself, if I'm going to Rock a thousand times with an empty lorry and passing Delabole quarry, where there's an abundance of slate and stone and blocks, I can carry a load back between Copplestone and Rock. So when I had a pound note, I'd buy sixty fourpenny blocks which could be used to build a house at Rock where building plots were for sale. I wanted a plot which was near an electric pole, not far from the water main, dry land with no rushes and close to the highway. I got what I wanted for £70 and then I was able to store the materials I was bringing from Delabole to Rock in my lorry. If I had a pound I could buy sixty blocks or if I had five shillings in my pocket, I could buy some wall stone. After some years when I had enough building material I got builders in to build my house. They said they'd never built anything like this before, there was so much material there – fourteen loads of china clay building sand, 5,000 blocks and seventy loads of wall stone. So the house in Rock was built, stone walls downstairs and block wall upstairs, as an investment for the future.

The sand was a Godsend to us farmers in those days. Under a magnifying glass you can see shells in it, washed in by the Gulf Stream and deposited here on the north coast of Cornwall. At Harlyn Bay there's sand that's richer still. The sand contains 9 cwts. of oxide of lime to the ton; here at Rock it's about 8 cwts. to the ton, that is about 40 per cent. The further inland you take sea-sand in North Cornwall, the more good it does. If you take this clean sand and spread it on the moorland grass and leave it, in time the stock will come from miles around to graze there. Wherever the sand goes on the acid soil, foxgloves and sorrel, furze, and devil's beard follow. The lime in the sand neutralises the acid and makes it fertile. There are dormant clovers in the soil. All they want is a little fertilisation by sea-sand and up they come. The red and white clovers are grand for fodder in the hay, with trefoil and rye grass to feed to the cattle and horses; that is why sand was so important in those days.

At Copplestone we grew wheat, barley, oats, mangolds, potatoes, turnips, cabbages, and rape. We had to have a certain amount of barley and oats to feed the livestock and the sheep would live on cabbages, turnips and mangolds. Some of the mangolds would be for the horses. The sheep would get fat on the rape.

We didn't use clean barley for feed, we mixed it with oats;

we called this mix dredgecorn. We also ground it up for pig meal or for the cows or horses. Our farm was 800 feet above sea-level, an inland farm. We didn't grow such good grain as farms below 700.

Not far away there was a stone mill with a water wheel where wheat could be ground. When Father and Mother were alive, Father ground his own wheat and mother had an earthware cloam oven to bake the bread in. Sticks were thrown in to heat the oven and the cinders raked out before the food went in to be cooked. In my parents' day the farm was self-supporting. When my brothers and I went back there we occasionally got the miller to grind some of our wheat for our own use, perhaps every few years, just to have the treat of home-baked wholemeal brown bread.

After I got married in 1939 I began farming at Tredole while my brothers ran Copplestone.

We sold mangolds to Delabole Quarry for their horses. Back in those days the quarry company would have eight or nine working horses. They'd be taking coal from the railway trucks to the boilerhouses.

There's an old saying 'Sheep are the rent-payers', so we sold our sheep each year. In the summer we'd have about eighty Devon longwool ewes, and they'd have eighty lambs. There would also be eighty to ninety yearling sheep – hoggets we called them – so when it came to dipping time in June, July or August, we had over 200 sheep to dip. The wool in those days would make above sevenpence a pound; during the depression we only got about threepence ha'penny or fourpence.

Again, smallholders in the neighbourhood were glad of a hundredweight or two of hay, or surplus straw which we'd deliver to them. The merchants at Boscastle who had horses and wagons to deliver their goods each had a team of big shire horses for which they bought hay, mangolds and straw for feed, so we had a market for our surplus. But the bulk of what we grew was consumed on the farm by our own stock. We kept a few hens, a donkey, and a goat which I used to milk.

Usually we kept ten or twelve cows. Sometimes we only had eight to milk. We made butter and supplied it to Mr Ward at Boscastle. He paid for it once a year when we settled up the farm bill, for linseed oil, timber, or a pot of paint or nails he had supplied us with. When we were settling up, he'd say '104 lbs. of butter at one and tuppence a pound – that'll come off your bill.' We also supplied the doctor with 3½ lbs. of fresh butter every week. Mother used to make quite a lot of butter in summer-time and if she had more than we had local demand for, she would sell it to another farmer for tenpence or tenpence ha'penny a pound, perhaps forty lbs. at a time. She used to make fancy butter for the Boscastle flower shows and at these shows I'd enter the jam I'd made. I won first prize for my gooseberry jam and beat eight women! Also second prize for blackcurrent jam at the same show.

The depression in the 1930s affected us considerably. Prices had been dropping year after year. As I said, the price of wool dropped. There's an old belief in Cornwall, why I don't know, that wool and tin go together. If the price of tin goes up, wool goes up. If tin drops, the price of wool drops. In the depression it fell below 1914 prices. My father used to sell oats and I delivered them to the mill for seven shillings a hundredweight.

When did the tide begin to turn in the farming world? Well, as a Cornish farmer I lost money from 1918 to 1933. These were the hard years. In 1933 we were just paying our way. Up till then it had taken us fifteen years to lose £1,100. It took us another fifteen years, from 1933 to 1948, to regain what we had lost. It meant we had worked thirty years of our lives virtually for food and clothes. Looking back, I'm glad I spent those odd pound notes and five shillings on blocks and stone for a house of my own when I retired.

It was not till 1937 that prices began to improve. Why? Because the government feared another world war. They thought if we weren't to be starved to death, we must improve our land. If you draw a line from the Cheviots down to Southampton, and cut out Wales, you'll find Cornwall and Cumberland are the two poorest counties on the west of England. What Cornwall needed for her soil was lime, phosphates and potash. I had brought 850 tons of sea-sand to spread on the land at Copplestone before the government gave us the chance to have a subsidy. I got no subsidy for that but later when I brought another 1,150 tons, I did get a subsidy. I got about half a crown a ton subsidy, 50 per cent of usual cost. When I took early potatoes to Plymouth, I'd go over to the lime-kiln and load up with either carbonate of lime or quicklime.

We had to let them know how much we had bought and the agricultural committee remitted half of the cost. That was the beginning of the improvement.

Prices for crops rose gradually. There was a steady improvement from 1937 onwards. During the Second World War, manures were rationed. We couldn't get enough to grow grass. The manure we were granted was to grow corn and potatoes. The grassland was getting poorer and poorer until after the war when we were able to get some basic slag to put on. The result was just what the soil wanted: phosphates. I had only four cows in 1939, but I sold milk to the Milk Marketing Board and it was then I started to make a bit of profit. I got two and fourpence a gallon delivered to the factory. We used to sell butter to a local fruiterer for one and fourpence a pound and he would retail it at one and sixpence a pound. That went on till 1942 when I got more cows, and sold untreated milk straight to the cheese factory at Davidstowe. They used to collect it in ten-gallon milk churns. I sold milk to the Board for twelve years from 1942 and had eleven cows when I finished. My total income over the twelve years was £4,383. That would be about £7 a week. It cost three pounds ten shillings to keep the cows, so I was getting about ten shillings a day for a seven-day week.

Once a year I asked my brothers, who farmed Copplestone, to come down to Tredole to do the milking and let me off for the afternoon for a British Legion outing. So I worked 364½ days a year. I had got a loan of £700 to pay the tradesmen to build the house in Rock but I paid that off. For the first seven years I hadn't to pay off anything; for the next seven years I paid £100 a year to clear the debt. It was never easy being a farmer's boy in the early nineteen hundreds but I've enjoyed my life.

When I came to live in my house in Rock I hadn't a pension, so I had to take a job for a bit, going on farms or weeding beet, gardening or taking a post round. Now I have a pension, and I'm better off than when I was working in the thirties.

Things were so bad in the twenties that I thought I should try to see farming in another part of the world. In 1928 I set off for New Zealand, via the Atlantic, Panama Canal, across the Pacific past the Galapagos Islands and Pitcairn Island and on to Auckland, New Zealand. I stayed in New Zealand for exactly 999 days. Believe it or not, I had seventy cousins in New Zealand, descendants of my great-uncle who went out from Cornwall about 100 years ago. I recently had a letter from my mother's first cousin out there and she's ninety-five. I did dairy-farming in New Zealand and learned quite a bit. I put what I had learned into practice when I came home. I worked on the farms of three cousins on South Island and also for a farmer who had Jersey cows and Southdown sheep. While he was on holiday in Fiji I looked after the farm, milked the cows and tended the sheep. One morning when I was there I experienced an earthquake. Suddenly there was an awful rumbling and shaking so that within a hundred miles no human being could stand upright. I could see the foreshore of the sea about a mile away gradually rising. It rose to a height of seventeen feet, and it has remained at that height to this day. Fish were left high and dry and the gulls came down and ate them up. I had taken a photograph of a certain spot there before the earthquake and I took another one after.

After New Zealand I went to Australia and worked on farms there – cattle, sheep and wheat farms. I only stayed there for six weeks, just to see it, but it was worth it. After that I went to South Africa and I was there for six weeks. I saw my uncle's grave where he had died serving in the Boer War.

I went down a gold mine, a thousand feet, and they let me dig gold just so I could say I'd done it! I'd like to have gone to the Victoria Falls but funds wouldn't run to that. On the way home at St Helena I had a cup of tea with the Bishop before sailing back to Southampton. I counted it up and I had been three years three months and three days absent from home. I came back to Tremorle, which my brothers had been farming while I was abroad. The total cost of my journey abroad had been roughly £100; £100 to go round the world; a penny a mile, board included. It cost £39 to go from Southampton to New Zealand in a four-berth cabin. If I had gone in a six-berth cabin, I could have done it for £37. It was £7 for a four-day journey from Auckland to Sydney and £2 from Sydney to Melbourne either by railway or boat. I went by boat because bed and board was included. Those three years and more of experience were worth the money. I knew a lot more about farming when I came back to Cornwall.

Cornish farmers had to be economical and hard-working in the early part of this century. I've been economical all my life because I was brought up that way. I had to look at a penny twice before I spent it once. You've got to face up to life. My wife who was a great support died some years ago.

I have many happy memories.

HARRY CHAMPION

Jobbing Gardener

For fifty years, interrupted by five years in the Army, Harry Champion was a jobbing gardener. He was wounded in the North African desert, but back in time to go on to Anzio, up through north Italy and finally across the Western Front to Hamburg – a dramatic contrast that has created both a philosophy and a character. He is now living alone in a council house in Rock, the village in which he was born in 1918.

The dominating influence in his boyhood was his grandmother who brought him up in a cottage that was once part of the old almshouses. She was a granite-like Cornishwoman who weathered the rearing of ten grandchildren of a family of nineteen. The rent for the cottage was twenty-five shillings for three months. Harry has keen memories of those days.

We used to pull Grandmother's leg when she was making the big pasties for ten of us. We told everybody she made them so big she had to put half in the oven and half on a chair and then turn them around! They made pasties of a terrific size in those days. Some years later I remember going up to the local bakery that was run by a Swiss chap. He was a good friend and he baked me a pastie for my birthday. It was thirty-one inches long and he laid it on a board for me. A farmer came in to the shop and said 'That's a lovely imitation pastie!'

I carried it out like a rifle on my shoulder. It was tied around with a little bit of string to save it breaking up. The first person I met was Miss Buse the schoolteacher. She asked me what I was carrying. I told her it was a pastie. She didn't believe it at first, so I put it on her garden wall and cut her off a corner with my knife. Yes, that was some pastie. Somebody said I should be in the Guiness Book of Records. I've eaten three pasties a day, seven days a week, for years. I still do.

My grandfather and grandmother were real Cornish

characters. Grandmother was a hard worker. She used to clean St Michael's Church and the Village Institute. She collected rabbit skins and rags for the cloth trade. She'd send these away on Monday mornings in the old bus. The driver would put her parcel on the train at Wadebridge and she'd have a cheque back from the millon a Friday morning. My grandmother also caught rabbits and skinned them.

Grandfather used to drive an old pony and trap; he was known to everyone as 'Nice Day' and I'll tell you why. The coal boats unloaded at Rock and the coal was stored on the quay. Grandfather would collect it and deliver it in his old trap. He had a real sense of humour. When it was raining hard, he'd put a coal bag over his head and the rain would run down his back and the muck would run down his face. To everybody he passed he'd shout 'Nice Day!' and people nicknamed him that for evermore.

The insurance man would come down to the old cottage once a fortnight. If my grandparents weren't there, he'd go straight to the old grandfather clock. I can see it now; you would never think it could tell you the time, for one hand was bent round one way and the other hand was bent the other. Anyway, stacked behind the pendulum were all the rates papers, insurance policies; everything. This fellow would just get the insurance policy, take the money on the table, sign the book and leave.

There was another old chap who worked on the Council and when he came to visit us he liked to get a dig in about the clock not being exactly on time. He liked to get at my grandfather. He'd arrive about one o'clock. Every day at two minutes past one, you could see the Padstow train crossing the bridge, and he'd come in at the door and say 'Clock's wrong again,' and Grandfather would retort, 'Don't be so daft, old Ben, it's the only thing right in this house.' But he'd put the clock right as soon as the train went over the bridge and old Ben had left.

When I left school I went to work in the neighbouring village of Polzeath for about fifteen shillings a week. I worked with another gardener who came to my rescue one day when I had raging toothache. I was in agony and the nearest dentist was in Wadebridge. I told this chap, and he said he would pull the tooth out. He took his pliers but they slipped off the tooth five times. Each time I put my head under the tap and washed my mouth out. In the end he got it out and I never felt a thing after; a back tooth and taken out with a pair of pliers!

I've spent most of my life gardening, mainly tending lawns and hedges. Constant cutting and occasional feeding, that's the answer. It's difficult hereabouts to get a good lawn – sandy soil all around. It dries up so quickly and you get a lot of old moss. You've got to watch it because a lot of people cut it too tight. If you cut the grass too tight and you have a fortnight's dry weather, up come the weeds. There's not enough grass to choke them. In good growing weather you should cut once a week.

When I cut the hedges, I use shears. Never use electric cutters. They're useless for some things. You take privet for example. To get a good privet hedge, you've got to start at the bottom. You clip and make a clear gap up four inches from the bottom. That way you can get your hand right in and pull up ivy or anything else, pull it right out. Then I come up the hedge and level in the sides. Instead of being square I level them in so that the top is narrower than the base. That way you can put a pair of steps up each side and reach both sides. Never let a hedge get out of hand. Start levelling when you get three parts the way to the top, if the hedge is about six feet. Maybe five foot is the best average height for a garden hedge and about three feet wide. That would give good shelter.

Wages have gone from fifteen shillings an hour to £2.50 or thereabout. So now a lot of people do those jobs themselves. Also people who have houses here but don't live here all year round get contractors to cut their grass, contract gardeners. So there's not the same work for the jobbing gardener on his own as there used to be.

I've done work for people like that. They come down maybe three days at Easter to their holiday house and, say, a week in the summer and they let the house the rest of the season and get good money. Sometimes when you give them a bill, and I've never over-charged in my life, they looked surprised. They don't realise the number of times you've had to do the cutting. In one house with a well in the garden where the gass grew strongly, it was oftener than once a week to keep it under control. From the end of March till the end of June, if you get a wet spell, you've got to cut every week or you're never on top of it.

After I came out of the army I got a job at St Enodoc golf course at about £2 a week. I did two years there as green keeper and caddy and learned to play. I did a round of the St Enodoc course in sixty-five. I still play. It doesn't matter where I go on Cornish courses, they still know me. I played recently in a Rotary competition. We raised £2,000 for a heart-testing machine that can be used in an emergency when the ambulance is called out. That was nice for it was the first one in the Wadebridge area.

Two princes from Thailand came during the war and married two English girls – Prince Bira who was a car-racing man and Prince Chula who ran the Home Guard here. There's a billiard table in the Rock Services Club now which was given by Prince Chula. I played with them and caddied for other well-known people, Carol Gibbons and Tony Jacklin among them. I played a lot of golf with David Astor, Nancy Astor's son. I expect to be playing with him when he comes down next month; his family used to own Brea House on the golf course. The Prince of Wales who abdicated used to play golf here; he was a nice fellow. When he came across on the ferry from Padstow he came up over the sand hills with an army of people marching behind him. I used to caddy a lot for Viscount Clifden of Lanhydrock and his sister Miss Agar Robartes, he was president of the club, which had fifty caddies.

Rock became popular as a holiday place and famous people came to stay or visit friends: George Robey who made famous the song '*If you were the only girl in the world*', Jack Buchanan and Kenneth Moore who would come down from London. There was plenty of stir then.

There have been big changes in the area from the days before and after the war. I admired the families who came to Rock and identified themselves with the Cornish, but now the planners have built up the place and there are many more new houses but there's not the social life that the real old Cornish community had. There are so many holiday houses empty for the winter months and so many people buy houses and then move on. The village has For Sale boards up all around. Years ago for instance we used to have a whist drive every week with

102

140 tables and we had dances every Friday night. Jock Lyneham from Oxford did a lot for the social and sports life; he was all for the locals. He'd have a cricket match in September and he'd bring a visitors' team with very good cricketers; one was a fellow who played for the Gentlemen against the Players and another fellow was opening bat for Worcester. Our side was Rock and St Minver combined. It was like a Test Match, and we had side-shows. At one time there were four lots of brothers who went to the same school, and some played for Rock and some for St Minver. Mr Lyneham also arranged a golf match with the caddies, after which we went to his house for soup and sandwiches and beer. Then they'd have a dance at the institute at Rock with a ladies' band and Mr Lyneham as the drummer. There was beer everywhere. We danced with whoever's partner we liked and pinched bottles of beer. It was good fun.

Another family who linked up with the local Cornish were the Bannermans. They came here on holiday very early in life – the father, Bertie Bannerman, and Nigel, Roger and Morton, all very good golfers. He bought Lowenna Manor and renamed it Dormie House. He ran it as a fine hotel. He had golfers there nearly all the year round. Commander Bannerman won the Cornish golf championship in 1937. The Bannermans were friends of Sir John Walsham whose house bordered the course. He was a great friend of Sir John Betjeman whose remains are buried in St Enodoc churchyard in the middle of the course.

Families like the Lynehams and the Bannermans weren't Cornish but they became involved with the Cornish and they were respected. I'm afraid too many 'foreigners' as they say here don't make that kind of effort now.

I'm sorry for the young people of Cornwall today. They haven't a chance of buying a house. People with money have come in and bought up second homes. It has ruined community feeling. The Council must take some responsibility. This little scheme I live in is fine; there should be more of them, as they would be within the reach of young Cornish men and women. I've been a lucky man. I've been happy in my work. It's been a good life.

MARY MAY

Cornish Housewife

Mary May was born in Truro in 1870 and died of cancer at the age of forty-nine. In that time she produced nine children. With no social services back-up and no modern conveniences, she set about coping, and fed and clothed her brood on her man's wage of fifteen shillings a week plus one shilling for overtime.

Norah and Lily, two of her daughters, tell her story.

Mother married John May, a farm worker, an expert with horses. In 1900 the couple came to Lanhydrock and in due course Father took charge of the heavy horses on the estate owned by Viscount Clifden. Mother had nine children, but Katie, one of us five sisters, died of tuberculosis.

We never felt poor; we were all fed and well clothed. Mother coped on sixteen shillings a week. How she did it we never knew. She never owed a penny to anyone at any time. She even saved a little each week from what she got from father. When Katie died, the butcher asked her if he could give her a loan to tide her over. She said 'No, thank you,' and the day after the funeral she gave father £5 to pay for the coffin. We always used to go out on Easter Sunday with new clothes. She was a miracle worker.

Mother made all the children's underclothes; quite an undertaking when you recollect that girls in those days wore chemises, vests, two petticoats, and knickers. She made little frocks as well, and boys' clothes, including their shirts. Her ingenuity was boundless. Flour came in cotton bags with the miller's name on them. She got the girls to wash and scrub the bags till the name was erased; then she would sew four bags together and the result was a white table-cloth or pillow slips. Every night when Father came home, he found his meal served on a starched, freshly laundered tablecloth made from flour bags. Mother kept a sharp eye on the boys' hobnail boots and girls' shoes and would regularly send them to the shoemaker to get metal caps and heels and toes.

She would go out and gather firewood in a wicker basket; we would do what we could to help. We girls would gather blackberries and snowdrops for the vicar in Bodmin and we'd get something for that. When the boys were about eleven or twelve they used to cut thistles for a local farmer. For each field they got half a crown which they gave to Mother.

In addition to these little extras Lily and I would get a shilling a week for keeping the Lanhydrock butler's wife company while he was with Viscount Clifden for the season in London. She was a nervous woman and didn't like sleeping alone. After school, when we arrived at her house she would give us supper; sometimes soup and rice pudding, sometimes stew. We would stay with her and before breakfast in the morning we would fetch her milk from the dairy in Lanhydrock House. After breakfast we'd set out for school, after handing the precious shilling over to Mother.

When we were about twelve and thirteen, Mother had to go into hospital and in the evenings a woman came to do the family wash. She received a shilling for this chore. We decided we would tell the woman that in future we would do the washing and put the shilling into the family kitty. Mother's guidance was paying off. Sharing became a habit and everything any of us was given outside was brought home. For example, after a children's party at Lanhydrock, Lord Clifden and his two sisters would stand in the doorway and give each child a large saffron bun. All of us took our buns home to Mother. We were learning that family life doesn't mean grabbing something for yourself.

A dearth of pennies there may have been; a dearth of food there wasn't. Few could teach Mother how to judge and buy meat economically. Her butcher gave her 'bits' and charged sixpence a lot. The neighbourhood abounded in rabbits which ended up on the table as rabbit pie, roast rabbit stuffed with parsley and breadcrumbs, and as stew. The family would receive the occasional game bird. Mother kept some hens and a few piglets which ultimately supplied fat and streaky bacon. She was an excellent baker and in addition to an endless supply of bread, fruit tarts and yeast cakes, there was always some special tit-bit on Sundays.

We remember the varied pasties made for our midday meal in the little school at Lanhydrock – beef and potato pasties, bacon and egg pasties, some filled with fruit, rabbit pasties supplemented with figgy rolls, raisins rolled in pastry. At lunchtime mother would carry a basket with the new-baked pasties half-way to school. When she saw us children come running to meet her, she would leave the basket on the ground and with a wave return to prepare Father's dinner. What the children couldn't eat was left in the playfield for the rooks, which swooped down when the school bell rang. A minor loaves and fishes miracle? Perhaps not so fanciful after all.

Our little sister Nora was sent to the small school at Cutmadoc when she was three and a half. This helped to free Mother for a few hours. Between the house and the school there was a long gentle slope and the boys used a board mounted on wheels to 'bus' the girls to school. That school 'bus' cost nothing in fares or petrol – a perfect DIY transport system except that the return journey from school to home made a greater demand on muscle-power.

Our memory of Father is of a kindly, moderate man, hardworking, with a passion for horses. But it was Mother who was our guiding light. Her love of reading and of books helped to feed the minds of her husband and family. Father found difficulty in reading and writing; perhaps today he would be diagnosed as dyslexic.

We still remember gathering round Mother when she read aloud to us before bedtime. She was a good reader. She read us books by Joseph Hocking, stories like *A Peep Between the Scenes*. We enjoyed all the stories. One memory stands out. Father had Charlie – one of our little brothers – on his knee. While he was listening to Mother reading, he was undressing Charlie, taking off his socks, and all the time the tears were rolling down his cheeks. The story was affecting him for he was very sentimental. Although he couldn't read or write he had a very clear brain, and he was proud of Mother's abilities.

After our bed-time story we had a drink of cocoa and a piece of yeast cake.

Every night Mother and Father would kneel beside their bed and say their prayers, but they never imposed religion on us children. We had religious teaching but that was in school once a week when someone came down from the vicarage to give us a lesson. Looking back, I think it was Mother who taught us all the right things.

I remember two fascinating incidents which illustrate Viscount Clifden's respect for our parents. When Katie was sixteen she became ill with tuberculosis. Viscount Clifden sent his Rolls to help get her to Plymouth as comfortably as possible. As the car carrying Mother and Katie approached the gatehouse, a woman came out. It was the Viscount's sister who had brought her fur coat to keep the ailing girl warm. Years later, when father was ninety and bedridden, the Viscount and his two sisters would visit him, bringing a bottle of brandy, a chicken and some fruit. I think these were gestures in recognition not only of service but of a quality of life which Mother and Father had brought to the estate of Lanhydrock.

Ladies' Maid at Lanhydrock

For over thirty years I was personal maid to two fine ladies, the Hon. Everilda and the Hon. Violet Agar-Robartes. They were the unmarried sisters of Viscount Gerald Clifden of Lanhydrock House. His father, the old lord, died two years after I came to Lanhydrock. I loved the family very much and they were very kind to me.

After the deaths of the family, Lanhydrock House has been run by the National Trust and they have done a fine job in preserving it and showing how the old Victorian household was run long ago.

Lanhydrock wasn't the only house owned by the family. There were Wimpole Hall in Cambridgeshire, the house at Wentworth, and the London house in Belgrave Square. I would go to London with the ladies. We never went to Clifden, the family's place in Ireland.

First of all we were at 37 Grosvenor Square, then we moved to 7 Belgrave Square. Princess Marina lived two doors below us. But the family loved Cornwall and we spent most time down here in Lanhydrock. We went up three times a year for the Buckingham Palace parties. The Queen and the Queen Mother came to the house and the Queen Mother and Princess Margaret came one day for lunch.

Wimpole Hall was a bigger place than Lanhydrock but Lanhydrock was much cosier and homely. We had the Queen Mother staying there. When we were at Belgrave Square in London, we didn't stay for weekends but went down to Wimpole Hall in Cambridgeshire. We'd go down on the Saturday and return to London on the Monday. His Lordship had his parties there for it was nearer London than Cornwall was. It was a wonderful place in Cambridgeshire with an avenue of two miles to the house.

The family would take me and a still-room maid from

Lanhydrock to Wimpole. They had a resident cook-housekeeper. We never took housemaids with us. The still-room maid would make the cakes and coffee and things like that. The resident housekeeper at Wimpole was a wonderful old lady. She used to go round in her black velvet bedroom slippers and she used to watch her housemaids. She would keep her eye on these girls but she couldn't say anything to me. There were valets there but the girls weren't allowed to go into the pantry where the men were. If she saw anyone going in, she'd say 'What are you going in for?' I remember one day I had to go into the pantry to give a message to the butler. She saw me coming out and said 'What are you doing in there, Evelyn?' 'Oh,' I said, 'I had to go in with a message, Mrs Jones'. She said no more. She was Welsh. There was a chapel in the house, a private one and outside there was a church.

We had a big staff at Lanhydrock in my time. When I came, there was a ladies' maid but at that time I was too young for that and I was under her. She was an elderly person and she died the year after I came to Lanhydrock. I used to help her pack for Miss Eva and Miss Violet and look after them and I learned everything I knew from her. When she died, the ladies took me on until they could get another maid. But they said I did so well for them they would like me to continue if I would. So I became personal maid to Miss Eva and Miss Violet. There had been talk that I was too young for the job but Miss Eva said 'No, she's not. She's looked after us so well.' I stayed with them to the very last.

They had rooms underneath mine. We were in the front and I just had the stairs to go down and was there when they wanted me, for I kept all their clothes and wardrobe. I was there when they wanted me, calling me with the bell.

I used to mend all their clothes and go up with them to London. Along with Mr Gerald, as he was then, they were as good as gold to me and they were happy days. Mr Gerald's father, the old lord, had been very old and died in his London home with two nurses looking after him. He was brought down here to Lanhydrock and lies in the vault where the family are buried.

The old lord had had a big family. Mr Tommy as everybody called him, the eldest, had been killed in the war.

Captain Alex had been in the Life Guards. Miss Eva had been a twin with Tommy. There were also Mr Gerald and Captain Cecil. Then there was Major Victor. As well as Miss Violet there was Miss Constance who didn't go into society much. She took up nursing and had a nursing home in Wimbledon. She'd come down every so often to Lanhydrock.

My ladies, Miss Eva and Miss Violet, were entirely different. Miss Eva the eldest was prim and proper and never did anything out of place, but Miss Violet was a scallywag. She loved horses, and would go riding. She'd come in and throw her suit off. 'Oh Violet,' Miss Eva would say, 'do be more careful!' But Violet was really very nice. She'd go to the drawers and say 'I want so and so Evelyn'. But I'd say 'Wait, I'll get it for you Miss Violet,' for she'd just turn everything upside down to find it.

While at Lanhydrock I was married to George, who was the chauffeur and valet to Lord Clifden. When we decided to get married we thought we'd have a quiet wedding. But what a wedding! It was in Lanhydrock Church. The family took it out of our hands and all the gentry came. There was a big reception in the House. There were sixty guests and his Lordship insisted on signing my certificate and off we went to Torquay for our honeymoon.

It was a funny thing about people's names. For instance my husband's real name was Cecil. But there was Captain Cecil; so as my husband's full name was Cecil George, it was decided to call him George. Then there was myself. I had always been called Eva in my own home. But of course there was Miss Eva in the house. So when I first went for my job, she said 'Have you got another name, my dear?' I said 'My name is really Evelyn'. So she said 'Would you mind if we called you Evelyn?' So Evelyn it was. It was the same with some others on the staff. The butler's name was Victor John, but as we also had Major Victor the butler had to be called John. Nobody seemed to use their proper names. But nobody worried for they were really wonderful to us and they were a family who'd do anything for anyone.

The war brought new experiences to everyone at Lanhydrock House. At that time there were four housemaids, four in the kitchen: cook, two kitchen maids and a scullery

26 Tom Dyer 27 Billy Johns

28 Bodmin Road Station, with water tank and branch line to Bodmin on left

29 Howard Mankee, awarded the British
Empire Medal

30 Howard at South Crofty
Tin Mine

31 Howard, when shift boss,
inspecting the mine

32   Jack Yeo at a presentation by his
     fellow workers on his retirement

33   Jack Yeo

34   There was little mechanisation when Jack started in the clay pits

35   Horses and waggons owned by Jack's relations. These took clay to port and on
     return from Par to Bugle the horses would get a drink of beer at The Norway Inn

36 Ships like these exported clay from Par early in the 20th century
37 Stan Yelland, with a clay shovel
38 William Chellew, a farrier in the First World War

39 The last blacksmith at St Minver

40 William, extreme right, with the tenor bell of St Endellion Church

41 The further part of the white building was the Chellew's home

42 Mr John Smith outside William's old smithy, which he saved from demolition

43 Competitors in a milking competition in the early 1900s

44 Jack Boney

45 Jack at Copplestone Farm

maid, and what you would call a charlady, the butler, two footmen, a hall boy and an odd man. My husband of course was chauffeur and valet. There was another chauffeur who did the shopping and the gardeners. I didn't have to go to the war but most of the maids went. My two ladies were in the Red Cross and they brought me work to do for that.

Miss Eva and Miss Violet decided they would have evacuee children. So Miss Violet went to the Memorial Club. She was supposed to bring back ten evacuees but she brought back seventeen. 'I couldn't leave them, Evelyn,' she said to me. 'Those two from the same family, we couldn't leave them apart.' So she brought an extra seven. We had seventeen and they were nearly all Catholics. They had a room above the Gatehouse for their services and a Reverend Father from Bodmin came over. The ladies loved them and took them on trips to the seaside. When the time came they didn't want to leave. Years later I had some come back to see me. I believe one lady said coming to Lanhydrock as an evacuee had changed her life.

In the happy days before the war the staff would go down to the library for prayers. There was a lovely organ in the library. Miss Violet would play and we'd have a hymn. Many of the old staff still alive say these were the happiest days of their lives. The family took an interest in them and often came to their help when they were in trouble. For a girl to get into service in those days in a great house like Lanhydrock was a good thing.

There were many dances in those days at Lanhydrock and also at Wimpole. At Lanhydrock of course there were dances in the house when the staff could bring a friend. At the end of a dance the girls would dash upstairs and get into their working clothes to clear the room for the grooms coming in for breakfast next morning. We had dances at the club at Lanhydrock. I had an acting box which I later sent to the Red Cross when it was finished with. It was full of Victorian things we would use for parties and dances. We used what was in the box to dress up. I went once as a Victorian Lady. You wouldn't have known me. I got first prize for that rig-out in three dances. Indeed the gentry liked it so well they got it photographed and framed and enlarged for me – an Early Victorian Lady. I've still got it. We would all go to the dances such as the Ambulance dance. The family would get tickets for us. We'd hire cars and all the staff go except perhaps the butler who'd wait at home at Lanhydrock. A key to get back in would be left for us. These were the happiest days of my life. You see, my mother died two years after I went to Lanhydrock and my father died the year before that so the family at Lanhydrock were more like my own folk than anyone else. When they went away for the weekend they'd say 'We'd never leave you Evelyn'. Upstairs and downstairs people were happy at Lanhydrock.

Christmas at Lanhydrock in the old days was a great occasion. It started with us going up to London ten days before Christmas to do all the shopping and get the presents in places like Harrods. We'd try to find out the kinds of things people wanted. I'd help with the ladies and John the butler would help with the men. Nobody was missed out and that included the gardeners. They were good to everyone. Then back we went to Lanhydrock.

At Christmas those who wanted would go to church, the church on the estate. I used to call Miss Eva before I went and then Miss Violet when I got back after church. They would go to the later communion. They'd have their lunch at one o'clock and we would have ours after that. Huge turkeys had been prepared for Christmas and everything to go with it.

On Christmas Eve we'd get our presents, one from the ladies and one from His Lordship. Just before six o'clock we'd get them. You should have seen the great hall decorated, with the beautiful tree the gardeners brought in. I'd go, then the cook and all the other women and then the men got theirs. On Christmas Day the family left everything to us. Everything was put in the dining-room and we helped ourselves.

At New Year the bell-ringers rang the Old Year out and the New Year in; then they'd come into the house for drinks.

When I came to Lanhydrock my husband George was second footman and had been there ten years before me. He learned to drive the Rolls and his Lordship wanted someone who could be both a chauffeur and valet. George drove the Rolls and looked after His Lordship's clothes and went off with him at weekends on business. He used to go to Bath or Newquay or Weston-Super-Mare or other places. He'd say to

George 'I'm going away this week-end'. Often this happened when there was a shoot on for he didn't like taking part when it meant anything being shot.

After His Lordship and Miss Violet died, I looked after Miss Eva at Lanhydrock. Then sadly she had a fall and had to be taken to hospital in Truro. She was there for three weeks and I went down there every day for she wouldn't let the nurses do anything for her. We wanted to get her home for we knew now there was nothing they could do for her. All the others had died at home and we wanted her to be there. We got her back to Bodmin hospital and she was there for a fortnight. George and I were with her every day. If she walked it was always on George's arm. George could have retired by then but Miss Eva always said 'You wouldn't leave me, would you, George?' He stayed till the very last. She died in hospital. They rang me one night and I was with her all day. She died next day and they buried her in the vault at Lanhydrock. Both she and Miss Violet were lovely people and they rest at Lanhydrock.

I remember towards the end when Miss Eva couldn't go to the hairdressers, I took on the care of her hair. I said to George 'I've never done this before' and George laughed and said 'You've taken on something, Evelyn.' We had always had our hair done in London by the ladies' hairdresser.

I went with the ladies to their other homes in London and to Wimpole Hall. They knew I didn't want to travel by air abroad but I'd see to all their packing and to their unpacking when they returned.

When Miss Eva was still alive, the National Trust only had part of the house and when she died George and I had to go down to Lanhydrock, for we had been given one of the best houses on the estate. We helped with the packing at Lanhydrock and a lot was given to the Red Cross. When Miss Violet had died, nothing had been touched in her room. Sadly we had only one Christmas in our house which Colonel Trelawny had after us. George had a coronary and they took him to Truro hospital. I didn't drive although we had a little car of our own but a neighbour kindly took me down. He was in the intensive care unit. When I got home I was worried because I didn't like the look of him. The bell rang and when I went to the door it was the police. He had died when I was coming home. It was a shock which I thought at the time I'd never get over. I lived in the house on the estate for several years, but it was a big place for me. Then they built this lovely flat for me near the House. It used to be the carpenter's shop. I remember they made me a drum here many years before when I went to a fancy dress dance at the House dressed as a drummer's boy. Now I live here happily almost within a stone's throw of the House.

Major Victor was made Lord Clifden after Gerald died. He had been living in Jersey and he would say to me 'You should come over, Evelyn, and stay at the villa.' It may be silly of me, but I never wanted to fly in a plane.

Lord Victor later went to live in another of the Clifden family's homes, at Wentworth, Virgina Water, a lovely place right on the golf course. I sometimes went there with Miss Eva for weekends from London, but more often we went to Wimpole Hall. Lord Victor once said to me 'It only takes an hour to go to Jersey, Evelyn. You'll be there before you can look around'. But no, he couldn't get me to go.

Lanhydrock has been my life. Like others who are still alive who worked upstairs-downstairs in the great house, I'd say these were our happiest days.

RICHARD AND ESME DAWE

Mayors of Bodmin

ESME DAWE

Mr and Mrs Richard Dawe have the unusual distinction of both having been Mayors of Bodmin and the couple's tireless work for the community came to a climax in 1980 when they were made Honoured Burgesses of the town of Bodmin.

Esme Dawe tells her story.

I was born in 1906, in the village of Constantine, six miles from Helston and seven miles from Falmouth. My father ran the village hotel, the Cornish Arms, for a brewery. I have vivid memories of those days, especially the annual dinner. You see, the Vyvyans of Trelowarren owned nearly all our village. Some people bought houses in the village with 'lives' on them. That means two or three people might have a lease on a house but after the last one died, the house would come back to the Lord of the Manor, Lord Vyvyan.

Every year when folk came in to pay their rent we had that dinner. We also used to take in lots of commercial travellers. They didn't have cars in those days and many of them came out from Helston by pony and trap. They might be travelling in groceries or for steel for the quarries, for ironmongery and so on.

A traction engine was used to haul the beer out to Constantine from Falmouth. The postman walked from Penryn, six miles off, delivering on the way. He'd arrive at the hotel, have his cheese and roll and then walk back to Penryn. There were no phones and somebody would get a shilling to run to a farm with a telegram.

My mother died when I was twenty-one and we moved into a cottage in the village. The bus started running to Helston and Falmouth and we got there for one shilling return. Richard

115

Dawe came to lodge with our family. In time he and I were married and moved to Bodmin.

I was always interested in people and in the community but I never thought I'd get as involved in the town's affairs as I did. When I lived in Constantine I was on the Church Council and did things like collecting for the nurses, taking part in flag days and having coffee mornings for various things but now I became really interested in the town's affairs. Dickie got on to the Council – and was elected Mayor three times. I went round with him as Mayoress and enjoyed it, so I thought maybe I should have a go! Little did I realise then just how much I was to be involved with the town's affairs. As a Cornish woman I felt I had a part to play.

In 1962 the Council elected me Mayor of Bodmin. From then on it was all go. In fact I don't think I ever stopped during the twenty-one years I was a councillor in Bodmin.

One of my first jobs was the mayoral procession, headed by the Town Crier, when I conducted the Assize Judge, Cornish-born Sir Archie Pellow Marshall, to the Assize service in the parish church. The traditional nosegay of herbs and flowers was always carried. In the old days this was to overcome the stench and smell of the prisoners.

As Mayor, I also took part in the old custom of 'Beating the Bounds'. Numbers of the townspeople would walk about twelve miles all round Bodmin, finishing up in the town. It was a proper day's outing, I didn't wear my mayor's chain that day, just ordinary outdoor clothes because we had to cross streams and wet fields, and half-way round we sat down and ate our pasties. At one point they would 'bump the Mayor'. This meant they lifted me and then bumped my backside on the ground. Twice we stopped to throw pennies in the streams for the children to pick up. Then I started the hurling, throwing a ball from one to another until we came back to Bodmin. Beating the Bounds is a good old custom; and Bodmin is a good old town, mentioned in the Domesday Book.

There was plenty of work to be done, for instance, supporting the playgroups and the old people. On Christmas Day we'd go round all the old folk. On one Christmas Day, we started at eight in the morning. It blew a gale and rained all day. We had to come home and change twice. There was a newspaper reporter with us and the water was running down the poor man's back. On Wednesdays I used to help the WVS in the canteen at St Lawrence's Hospital. What a difference now from the old days when some mentally-ill patients had to be locked up in padded rooms and slept on wooden beds with straw paliasses. On Thursday I had coffee mornings in the Shire House for different people, like policemen's wives or the Mothers Union. Then there was the crowning of the Carnival Queen and also we'd go round and inspect the council tenants' gardens and there was a prize for the best kept garden. I had to attend many bazaars and fêtes. I spent all my time meeting people and I liked that because I'm interested in people. There's good in everybody. I once had a chat with Prince Charles and another time with Princess Alexandria when she visited St Lawrence's Hospital. There was one old lady there who was a hundred years old; she'd been in the mental hospital for sixty-six years, looked after all that time.

RICHARD DAWE

Dickie Dawe, husband of Esme, was born in 1895 in Liskeard. In 1925 he came to Bodmin as a boot and shoe repairer. His memory like his wife's is as vivid as ever.

When I came to Bodmin I set up in an old shed in Crockwell Street. It was mostly repairing work, although I did make special shoes for some people, such as cripples, people with bunions and so on. Previously I worked with my brother who was a shoemaker at Padstow. He was expert at making shoes. He could make a pair of leather boots in a day. I worked from half-past seven in the morning until nine at night. At that time a good pair of shoes cost a few shillings.

I rented a shop and employed a man to help me and later moved to Fore Street. The rent was £3 a week. My friends said I was a fool to pay that money. But I was not afraid either of a challenge or of hard work. So much so that later I was able to buy the shop. By then I employed three people. Eventually I bought Treverton's business and Mrs Kendall's business and added them to my own property, making one big shop.

When I started, a pair of shoes cost, as I said, a few shillings. In about the 1960s when I sold the shop to the Co-op, they still only cost £3 or £4. Look at the prices now! Yes, when I came to Bodmin, you could have got a really good pair of shoes for twelve shillings and eleven pence and a pair of rubber heels fixed on cost one shilling and threepence in the old money. I used to repair all the staff's shoes from Viscount Clifden's estate of Lanhydrock. I remember once Lord Vivien of Glyn came in with a pair of old riding boots and asked me to put a patch on one side of a boot and he waited in the shop while I was doing it. He had been wounded in the South African war. He was very interested and pleased with the job.

During the Second World War four thousand Americans came to the town. They were good for trade. They used to buy the best brown boots for ordinary street wear. They got permits from the officers to buy what they wanted. They were good customers.

But we sold mostly ladies' shoes during the war, because so many men were called up. My staff were kind and always ready to serve. My senior woman trained them in how to be helpful. You don't always see that nowadays. We had many a good laugh. There was an errand boy who was keen to ride a bike. We had one of these tradesmen's bikes with the carrier in front to hold boots and shoes. We used to send them out on approval, for we knew everybody and we could trust people. Anyway, this boy was thrilled to bits to use that bicycle. One afternoon he was away much longer than usual, and very late coming back. I asked him where he had been. 'Mr Dawe', he said, 'I think I must have fainted.' A few days later a friend happened to say that he had seen my bike at Polzeath. The lad couldn't resist the temptation to ride the bike to the seaside. He hadn't fainted, he'd been enjoying himself beside the sea! As I say, it was a small friendly place and if people hadn't the money, they just paid us in instalments when they had anything to spare. Sometimes people would pay to have their boots or shoes soled and they'd not come back to pick them up, so after a bit we took them to jumble sales. This happened with evacuees during the war. Some just went back to London because they were bored, with no excitement or fish and chip shops. They'd sooner be among the bombs than be bored stiff down here.

I must have caught Esme's early enthusiasm for community work. My activities were as varied as hers. I was a founder member of the Rotary Club in Bodmin, and I liked to visit the elderly in hospitals or old people's homes on birthdays or wedding anniversaries. I was elected town councillor, an office I was to hold for thirty-three years, twelve years longer than my wife. I became Mayor in 1956 and again in 1957. I completed the hat trick in 1968.

OWIE JEWELL

Shopkeeper

'A jewel in Bodmin's Crown.' That's how a fellow-townsman with an ear for an apt if obvious pun describes Howard Jewell, retired radio, TV and electrical dealer in Bodmin. But to most folk he is affectionately known as Owie.

When you meet Constance Jewell, whom Owie married in 1926, and especially when you meet them together, you realise the quality of their teamwork. It is this teamwork which in sixty years of marriage has released the positive energies, the quiet humour and the compassion of the Cornishman. In the family are two children, four grandchildren and three great-grandchildren.

Whatever he may think, there is something special about octogenarian Owie. It began to show when he was thirteen. One day near the beginning of World War One, Owie set out for Lanhydrock with three of his pals. It was autumn and the chestnuts hung heavy on the trees in Viscount Clifden's estate. The other boys were the sons of a police sergeant, a parson and the assistant station-master in Bodmin, men in those days of some standing in the community. Owie's father was a hospital attendant. The relationship of father and son was a healthy one, based on mutual respect and earthy common sense. The lad did not get away with anything but Owie says his father was just and fair. Here is his story in his own words.

On this occasion my three pals and I found ourselves within Lanhydrock estate, gazing in admiration at a giant chestnut tree laden with every schoolboy's dream. Glancing round and not seeing anyone, we decided that two should climb up into the tree while the other two stayed on the ground to collect the fallen chestnuts and keep watch.

The police sergeant's son and I were standing at the base of the tree but I'm afraid our watch wasn't very good. We turned round and saw a gentleman with a small dog approaching us. We thought it must be His Lordship himself.

120

We warned the boys up the tree to keep quiet and we pretended to walk round the tree. His Lordship came over to us and asked what we were doing and we said we were going on a ramble to Restormel Castle. 'Yes', he said, 'But what are you doing here by the tree?' We told him we were just looking up the tree. He knew, of course, this was not the whole truth and he asked if there was anyone up the tree. This caused us to hesitate quite a time. My friend, the policeman's son, was a very nervous type of boy and he didn't say anything so I said 'Yes, there are two friends up the tree.' He asked them to come down and they did. He said it was wrong to climb trees on the estate without asking permission and he wanted to know our names. Of course we gave him our names correctly. Then he asked who our fathers were. At this, the others were upset because the boy who was the parson's son knew his father would be annoyed and the other boy whose father was a police sergeant at head office also knew his father would be angry, although he had not actually been up the tree. Although the third boy didn't need to worry quite so much about his father's position, he knew his father would be very angry with him for getting into trouble.

I felt it was different with me. I had a wonderful father and I knew he would accept whatever I told him as being the truth. He was also the son of a cattle-dealer and therefore a countryman. So I thought I should take the blame.

I explained to His Lordship that it would be serious for these boys and they would get into very severe trouble when they got home if it was found they had been stealing or taking things that didn't belong to them. And while my father would remonstrate with me and certainly scold me and tell me it should never happen again, I didn't think it would affect his job as it might do the others. His Lordship thought a bit and then agreed that he wouldn't get in touch with our fathers, and we were naturally pleased about this. Then he said to me that it was right and proper for me to say what I did and that any time I was coming to Lanhydrock and wanted chestnuts, I was first of all to come to the house, tell my name to whoever answered the door, and permission would be given for me to have chestnuts and go through the park. I never forgot my first meeting with Lord Clifden and curiously enough, neither did he.

121

I started work in a garage, and when the viscount's chauffeur was in his town house in London or if something was wrong with his Rolls Royce, he would ask me to drive him to Newquay where he was a director of some hotels. I always had the same food as he had and he would come into the steward's room of the hotel before I started my meal and make sure it was in accordance with his order. When Lord Clifden died, my relationship with the new viscount was equally warm.

It is strange how a chance meeting can affect your life. That certainly was the case with me because old Lord Clifden always took an interest in what I was doing. After working in the garage I got a cycle shop of my own. Lord Clifden had a large family of boys and girls and he got all their bicycles from me. They bought their radios from me too when I took over the shop and began to sell electrical goods and radios and later television sets.

I well remember one incident that concerned television. Lord Clifden owned a house in Belgrave Square in London and he wanted a set installed there and an aerial mounted on the roof. I told him I'd get the firm who supplied me from London to install the set and the aerial. He was quite happy about this and I was relieved as I've no head for heights. But when I got the bill from the firm I was dismayed because they charged about six times more than I would have charged if I had done the job myself.

However I settled with them and then went to see Lord Clifden. I explained to him apologetically but he just wrote out a cheque for the amount and gave it to me. Then he gave me some advice.

'You're in business to make a fair profit,' he said. 'You've always got to make sure you do this. Now I'm going to give you what I think would have been a fair profit on this transaction.' His sound advice was as helpful as his kindness.

Saturday, 14th April, 1984 set the seal of a lifetime on my busy life. A crowd gathered inside and outside the public rooms in Bodmin. The Mayor accompanied by the Town Crier, town officials, the High Sheriff of Cornwall, Chairman of North Cornwall District Council, family and friends processed to the accompaniment of the town band. They were processing as the official programme indicated, to 'the

Conferment of the Distinction of Honoured Burgess upon Edward Howard (Owie) Jewell, Esq.'

The national anthem preceded the ceremony of acceptance and after speeches illuminating my career, the Honoured Burgess was invited to sign the roll of honour and accept the framed certificate.

I suppose I got this honour because I always enjoyed being involved in the town's affairs. I was a founder member of the Bodmin Rotary Club, and was twice elected president, and I was also the founder president of Bodmin Round Table. An enthusiastic angler, I was a founder member of the Cornwall River Board and a Conservator of the River Camel. My personal angling experiences in the Camel estuary from boyhood fitted me for my advisory services to the River Board. I was president of the Bodmin Angling Association for many years and a life member of Rock Angling Club. Within the Police I was a special constable from 1939 to 1964, where believe me, it needed some wit to oil many a stressful situation.

I have been made a serving brother of St John's Ambulance Brigade which I joined as a driver in 1919, and I have always been interested in the health of the community especially in those at either end of the age spectrum, particularly those who are both sick and elderly. I've been a long serving member of the League of Friends of East Cornwall Hospital where I've had great fun in acting as Father Christmas since the 1960s. I'm also one of the Friends of the Athelstan House Old People's Home.

I've done my best to encourage the sport of football in the area. I'm a life member of the Bodmin Town Amateur Football Club and was its secretary for seventeen years. I've held the posts of president of the Bodmin and District Football League and president of the East Cornwall Premier League. It's always been a great pleasure being involved with young people. Then they made me president of the Bodmin Gardening Association. I've lost count of all the things I've been involved in over the years. If you love a place, you can't help getting involved. I love Bodmin; it is part of me and I've never wanted to live anywhere else.

JOHN CORIN

Bank Manager

John Corin's grandfather was a retired naval officer who became a coastguard officer at Coverack. John Corin of Coverack, an octogenarian, spent all his working life at Barclays Bank in Cornwall. His ambition as a boy was to become a sailor but due to inadequate eyesight his life took another direction. His brother went off to the Merchant Navy in 1916. His father was coxswain of the old Coverack lifeboat. The family's roots go back in Cornish history to the thirteenth century and indeed, in the years before the Napoleonic Wars one of his ancestors was John Corlyon, a very successful smuggler. John Corlyon's story is typical of that of many Cornishmen of previous centuries and is graphically told by his descendant.

John Corlyon was apprenticed to a boat builder at Devoran and then came to Coverack to build boats. He was a big man, six foot two inches tall and seventeen stone in weight, who could build a fifteen-foot boat on his own. He was also ambitious and finding that he could not make a living as a boat builder, he took off for Roskoff in Brittany, where he made contacts and commenced his career as a smuggler.

He soon gathered a team around him to bring brandy, gin, tea, silk and so on into Cornwall. Tea was in great demand and he could usually bring it in and sell it for a quarter of the usual price. Eventually he owned a sailing schooner and had a crew of eight.

He lived in a cottage in Coverack near where I was born, which was bombed by the Germans in the last war. Everyone in the village and the farmers and the crew knew what John Corlyon was doing, and helped him to keep out of the way of the customs men. If anyone saw a suspicious looking stranger in the area they would get word to John's wife. If he was out at sea he would look through his telescope to the clothes line on the high ground behind his cottage. If there was no danger he would see pegged out his famous red shirt – the sign that the customs men or the strangers had gone. If there was no shirt on the line he stayed out at sea or landed at one of the other little coves along the coast.

If a smuggler was caught he was press-ganged into the Navy but a smuggler was also a trained sailor so they prized and promoted him. John Corlyon was caught in Mount's Bay and locked up in St Michael's Mount. He escaped but was caught again and taken to Plymouth and trained in naval arms. He fought at the Battle of Algiers under Lord Exmouth.

In the old days smuggling was really a great industry. The smugglers brought all sorts of luxuries to Cornwall, which the people would not otherwise have had. There was a young schoolmaster who started a little private school at Polperro. He wasn't having great success so being a man of some education he started keeping accounts for some of the smugglers. He did very well at this, for there were lots of smugglers at Polperro, and he became their financial adviser. As a result he started a bank and became a most respected member of the community. He made so much money that he eventually owned the harbour at Polperro. So you could say it was smuggling that encouraged early banking there.

In those days banking was closely related to the main industries in the county. Banks started up to serve local interests such as the mining companies in Redruth, Camborne and St Just; fishing in Penzance, St Ives, Mevagissey, Looe and Padstow; and farming in the inland areas round Truro, Helston, Liskeard and Bodmin. It was usually a leading man in a particular industry who started a bank.

An example of this is the Bolitho family. They were in mining and they also provided money for boats and nets in the pilchard fishing industry. They started a bank in Penzance. They opened another branch at St Ives, another in Newlyn and another in Porthleven. Then there was a Mr Foster who was interested in agriculture. He started a bank in Bodmin and another one in Lostwithiel. Mr Coode started a bank in St Austell with a branch in Mevagissey where there was a lot of pilchard fishing and whence pilchards were exported to Italy. There was also a Mr Grylls who had a bank in Falmouth and Mr Willyams who started a bank in Truro. Eventually all those people came together and combined to form a bank which was known as Bolitho, Foster, Coode, Grylls, Willyams and Company. They thought this was too long a name and altered it to the Consolidated Bank of Cornwall. This bank joined Barclays Bank in 1905; I should say Barclays joined the Cornish bank because the Cornish don't like the idea of being taken over by anybody. Lloyds came down to Cornwall and took over the Capital and Counties Bank, based mainly in Truro but also with branches all over Cornwall. Barclays and Lloyds had in those days the bulk of the business. When I first entered Barclays there was no Westminster Bank in Cornwall. The Midland, known as the London Joint City and Midland Bank, came about 1919.

I applied for a job in Barclays Bank in 1923 but as there were no vacancies my name was put on the waiting list. Three months later I got a letter to say I should go to Penzance for an interview with Colonel Bolitho, who was a bank director in charge of the whole of Cornwall. He interviewed me, and he told me to come back to Penzance the following Saturday to have a medical examination. Then he said he would decide whether or not to offer me a job. After the medical I got a letter to say I could start as the new junior clerk at Bude branch on 1st August and I would be on probation for six months.

There was a little personal thing about my interview I always remember. In those days you had to sign what was known as the Fidelity Agreement. But as I was only seventeen I wasn't legally old enough to enter into the agreement so my father had to sign the document as well as me, and would be released when I became twenty-one. I was told to go to Helston branch to sign the agreement as Helston was the nearest branch to Coverack. The manager at Helston was a well-known and brilliant man. He was a local Methodist preacher, so I had a little sermon from him at the start. He told me that I should qualify myself for promotion, explained my duties to the bank, and said that everything that happened in the bank was confidential – which was good advice. Then he explained the document to my father and me. He took up his pen – it was in the days when we used inkwells – and handed it duly dipped in the inkwell, to my father. My father was a fisherman; he had been to the village school and his writing was really copperplate. My father signed and gave the pen back. The manager looked at the pen and looked at me and put the pen down. I remember to this day the thought that went through my mind, 'The miserable old so-and-so isn't going to let me use his pen.' Then he pressed a bell and in came the junior clerk who was told to fetch a pen for me to sign with. The junior clerk protested that there was one on the desk. The manager said sharply, 'I know that but I told you to get a pen.' The chap hurried out and came back with another and gave it to me. It was then that I made a resolution that whether I ever achieved a managership or not, I'd always let a young lad use my pen.

In the course of time I became manager of the Hayle branch and later of the Helston branch where I sat in that same chair. By that time girls were being interviewed as well as boys. I'd get their examination results, 'O' levels or 'A' levels or both, and I'd send these to the local head office together with my opinion of the youngster and finally they would be interviewed – still by a member of the Bolitho family. If a youngster was offered a job and took it, then I had this little ceremony to go through. I'd explain the document to the father and son or daughter. I'd take out my own fountain pen, take the top off and offer it to the father and then to the youngster. Funny how you can remember for ever a little thing like that, that had made an impression on you in your youth.

I started my career in Bude in the early twenties. There were only four of us. In a very small branch there might be only two at one time; the manager and the first cashier. In Bude all four were men – indeed I worked for eight years before I worked in a branch with a woman in it. At that time we were just changing over to typewriters. When I was at Bude tourism was beginning and cars were just coming in.

There wasn't so much money about in those days and there was a different attitude towards it. People, by and large, didn't think of borrowing. The biggest part of the country banking business was savings; people with deposit accounts. Ordinary people would try to save a bit to cover themselves in case of sickness or if a member of the family died, so they'd have money to deal with it. People liked to feel their money was safe. I've a wonderful memory of one small branch I moved to. The cashier told me they had an elderly lady who came in every month. She'd come to the counter and say, 'Good afternoon, can I see my money please?' When she said that, I would say to

127

one of the lads at the back, 'Show Mrs X her money'. He would go into the strong room and pick up a £100 bag of silver or a £5 bag of coppers which weighed the same and he'd come back to the counter and hold it up for the lady to see and she'd say, 'Thank you, good afternoon'. She believed that we kept everybody's money in separate bags in the strongroom!

I've vivid memories of those early days in my first job. Above me were the manager, the cashier and the ledger clerk. I was the junior. As the junior I answered the telephone and dealt with the post. The manager wrote letters in longhand in copying ink, for there were no typewriters at that time. He'd take the letter and put it under a transfer sheet with a sheet of blotting paper on top. These would be put between books in a press. When you did this you hoped to goodness you hadn't blotted the manager's writing. You weren't very popular if you had to tell him you'd blotted his letter. I also dealt with all the cheques drawn on other banks. Each day cheques would be sent off by post to the clearing house in London. I was really a general dog's body. If anyone out of town rang up and asked for their pass-book, it was my job to write it up and send it off.

When I started in Bude I got £60 a year. Of course I had lodgings to pay. But farm workers were only getting about seventeen shillings and six pence a week to bring up a family on. By comparison I wasn't too badly off. It was a job I liked. It was pensionable and I was quite happy. It was a good job for a lad who had what we called in those days the school cert. It was a job which, although I didn't realise it then, helped you to give something to the community in voluntary services that were worthwhile.

Banking practices when I was in my first job were very different from what they had become by the time I retired. The ordinary people, as I've said, had deposit accounts. Remember there was no social security then. When Lloyd George later brought in the old age pension it was, I think, five shillings a week. For the people banks were mainly for saving. They'd drop their hat on the counter and they'd produce their deposit pass-book and in early January and early July they'd come in to get their interest. Even a lot of business people who were doing a deal with somebody would pay in cash. The habit of having a current account and a cheque book was only just starting. There was more integrity in those days too and there weren't the burglaries, hold-ups and robberies there are today, but people were beginning to realise it was a lot more convenient to carry a cheque book than to carry a bag full of money. When the sovereign went out during the First World War, the banks still kept the scales at the counters for weighing them because they believed they would come back after the war, but they never did. It was nearly all ten shilling notes and pound notes. You wouldn't see many fivers but now the fivers and tenners have taken over.

We must remember people didn't need to borrow so much. There was a lot of poverty but things were so much cheaper than they are today. Even a mere twenty years ago, in the 1960s, you could buy a farm of say eighty acres for about £5,000 or £6,000. The same farm today would cost up to £120,000. You could buy a good cow then; I am talking about twenty years ago; for £50 or £60. Today the same animal would cost ten times that amount. A tractor with implements would cost £1,700. The money values are totally different.

In my early days lending money to farmers was mainly in the transactions of running what is a seasonal business. It might be a case of a farmer buying ten or twelve young bullocks which would be ready for market in six months and he would want a loan just until he could sell them. Or a man had three lovely fields of broccoli coming on which he'd be sending to market in January or February and we'd give him a loan to tide him over until then.

I remember a very humorous incident concerning my uncle when he was eighty-five and myself who was then about forty-eight. He was vice-chairman of the Coverack lifeboat committee and, presumably, in the running for chairman. After I had been their auditor I was asked to join the committee. One day a committee member said to me, 'Next month at the annual meeting the chairman is retiring. We admire your uncle but we think at eighty-five he's a bit too old to be chairman. Would you take it on?' I chuckled and told him this might cause a family feud, but finally I said I would. Then, at the meeting, the squire was elected president and I was nominated and seconded as chairman. My uncle was re-elected as vice-chairman. He didn't say a word till we came out of the meeting. We were walking up to where he and my mother lived in the little cottage above the green by the entrance to the harbour. He suddenly stopped dead in his tracks, his pipe in his mouth, leaning on his walking stick, and said, 'I don't know why they elected a boy like you as chairman.' It was his way of telling me I didn't know anything about it, him being eighty-five and me a mere forty-eight.

In addition to all the offices I've mentioned I was always involved in affairs connected with the Methodist Church. Things have changed a lot in many parts of the country now with regard to bank managers. The motor car has contributed to the change. When I was a branch manager in a town, I was expected to live in that town, take up treasurerships and mix with the local people, so that I was identified with the local community. Today, many of the managers don't live in the town where they work; they live out in the country and drive in every day.

I have had a lifelong interest in the history of Cornwall, particularly in the tales of seamen and smugglers. I don't go along with all that's said about the wreckers. I think it has been grossly exaggerated. All coastal people at heart are sailors, and when sailors are in trouble they help each other. But with regard to smuggling, yes, it took place in a big way. In the old days the Cornish, being Celts, were much allied to the Irish, the Welsh and the Bretons. It's interesting that many of the churches on the south Cornwall coast are called after Breton saints. For instance the most southerly church in the British Isles, Landywednacks, is named after a Breton saint. On the north coast many of the churches are named after Irish saints. Cornwall has a very long coastline and the people have always traded with the Welsh, the Irish and the Bretons.

Cornish boats would go across to Brittany to buy brandy, gin, tea, silk, good quality gloves and clothing luxuries which rich people were willing to pay for. Suddenly from London came word that if these luxuries were brought into Cornwall, there would be an enormous tax imposed on them. This applied also to Devon and other counties for there was smuggling all over the south coast. As we are only eighty miles from Brittany smuggling thrived in these parts. I've mentioned the activities

130

of my ancestor, John Corlyon; everybody in Cornwall was in the game, especially the wealthier people who could buy the stuff. The magistrates, who were usually local squires, and the better off members of the community, let the smugglers go scot-free or found them not guilty. There was the feeling that the real rogues were those in London, who imposed the taxes. The smugglers who were caught by customs men from up country were usually press-ganged into the Navy.

My ancestor, John Corlyon, was a staunch Methodist and an admirer of Charles Wesley, as were some of his fellow-smugglers. When they were in Brittany they would sometimes hold a Methodist service on the quay while their boat was being loaded with smuggled goods.

FRANK HARVEY

Doctor on Call

Dr Frank Harvey practised medicine all his professional life around the Camel estuary. He was the son-in-law of Dr Marley who practised in Padstow. Dr Marley's father was Dr William Miles Marley, a great friend of Charles Dickens who adopted Miles Marley's name for his ghost in *A Christmas Carol*. Dickens told his friend it would be a household name 'by Christmas'. Miles Marley was noted for his interest in women's and children's illnesses and he was honoured by Heidelberg University in Germany. One of his patients was the famous Tom Thumb (Charles S. Stratton), whom Barnum brought to Britain. In 1846 a newspaper described Stratton as a perfect miniature man only 31 ins. high, perfect and elegant in his proportions and weighing only 15 lbs. Dr Miles Marley spent his last days in Port Isaac. He is buried in St Endellion cemetery. Obviously Frank Harvey inherited a strong medical tradition through his family connections.

He was born in Linkinhorne in North Cornwall in 1866. His parents died when he was very young and an elder sister brought up the family. A pupil of promise, he went to school in Plymouth and from there to the Middlesex Hospital, London, to begin his medical studies. He returned to Cornwall, to his first practice in Padstow, and never left it. He began his professional career in an area of close friendships and relationships and married one of the eight daughters of Dr Marley. The family home was where the Bird Garden now is in Padstow.

His was a general practice in a scattered area of countryside and estuary, from Stepper Point to Wadebridge and across the estuary to Rock and its farming hinterland. In Victorian times, doctors were much thinner on the ground, so it was a twenty-four hour day job, calling for physical and mental toughness. Before they had cars, reaching patients, especially at night, was no mean feat in itself.

Dr Harvey had a surgery in Rock and used the ferry to get there. If the sea was rough he had to do a fourteen mile detour via Wadebridge by horse and trap. In the days before the telephone, the problem of communication was crucial. For instance, if someone in Rock became ill at night, a fire would be lit on the sand which could be seen across the estuary in Padstow. Whoever saw it immediately contacted the doctor who called out the ferryman. If the patient was in one of the farms, usually a horse and cart would be waiting on the beach for him. A fire was never lit unless it was felt to be really necessary.

Until recently there lived in Rock a Cornishman who used to work the threshing machines on the farms. Tom Champion used to remember running down the beach to light the fire that would bring Dr Harvey across the estuary. (He also remembered the day in 1927 when the Prince of Wales spent the night in the Hotel Metropole in Padstow and came to Rock to play golf and it was Tom who was his caddy.) Tom said the doctor was one of the best.

For inland areas there had to be other means of communication. People used to hang out red handkerchiefs on sticks at their garden gates to attract the doctor's attention when he was in the area. He usually visited Rock twice a week. In the scattered hamlets and villages, there was a sense of community which ensured news of illness was passed on as quickly as possible. The danger of a serious medical emergency was always a real one because doctors in those circumstances had very limited facilities and resources, and only minor operations could be performed within the practice. Dr Harvey had a small surgery in Wadebridge to cope with patients in that area and normally he would go there twice a week.

In his limited leisure time he loved fly-fishing and shooting. Many of the farmers who were his patients let him shoot on their land.

Adela, his wife, complemented her husband's work by her interest and involvement in local affairs. Tablets in the church commemorating the committed lives of her own parents and later those of her husband and herself are a reminder of what they did for the folk around them. When Dr Harvey was setting out to visit a woman patient, Adela would make up a posy or bunch of flowers for her to give that extra bit of cheer. She'd take bowls of soup down to the alms-houses and would often visit patients to offer them her support. Her daughter, Enid, remembers staying with a friend near Padstow once, when a workman came to the house to do some job or other. He had his hands behind his back, holding a bunch of flowers. He gave them to Enid explaining 'I want to thank you for what you sent with the doctor when my wife was ill. I've been waiting years to say that and to give you these.' 'It wasn't me, it was my mother,' Enid told him, but she was very grateful to him.

Mrs Harvey always looked forward to the ancient Padstow 'Obby 'Oss (Hobby Horse) festival held annually on May Day. A succession of townsmen squeeze inside a large caricature model of a horse and carry it in procession round the town. The day is marked with singing and dancing, conviviality, merriment and let it be whispered, a certain amount of horse-play, when people might get a wetting in the harbour. Enid remembers 'they would come and dance outside our house, then the 'Obby 'Oss would come to the front door, and Mother would come out to shake hands. A hand would emerge, from a hole underneath the long protruding neck of the horse. The 'Oss had to squeeze sideways to get in through our gate. After the First World War, they started another horse called the 'Peace 'Oss'. In the evening they both danced round a maypole.'

Rock, the lovely village opposite Padstow, was always a favourite with Dr Harvey and his family of two daughters. The girls spent hours on the sands and along the rocks and beach, for they went on holidays across to Rock. Enid, now in her ninetieth year, lives permanently in Rock, in Stoptide Cottage, a name that speaks for itself. After Dr Harvey's death in 1940, Adela came from Padstow to live with Enid and died in Rock at the age of 101 years and 10 months. She had enjoyed life to the full as the wife of a busy Victorian and Edwardian country doctor. During the First World War, Enid worked at Watermouth Castle in Devon, a home for convalescent officers which she described as 'almost like one big family party.' After the war in 1919, she returned to Padstow and cared for Dr Harvey and his wife until their deaths.

What kind of place was Victorian Padstow? What sort of medical practice was it? Enid said:

My father's practice was not a lucrative one. He realised that many of his patients couldn't afford to pay a bill, so he didn't send them one. They couldn't afford anything extra.

Padstow was mainly a fishing town. There were changes in the patterns of fishing. Originally pilchards were the main catch but their shoals moved away and herring became the prime target. I remember the Scots girls coming down to Padstow to gut and prepare the herring. There was a place where sawdust was burned and herring were smoked over it. Some girls came from Arbroath, the home of the famous Arbroath Smokes which are as well known in Scotland as the Cornish pasties are in England. When the herring in turn left our coasts, the steam trawlers went out for deep-sea fishing. Sometimes when it was very stormy you'd get fifty sheltering in the harbour at one time. The first trawlers had sail. They were a fine sight as they steamed out of the estuary. My father had many patients and many friends among seamen and fishermen and their families.

A Padstow man born in 1905 told me that in his youth Padstow was a busy seaport town. In my father's day there were three boat-building yards. Seafaring men would come back to Padstow to their homes and migratory seamen would land there when their ships called in. There was a lot of drunkenness and misery and poverty. An open stream ran down from near the church to the harbour and people would throw sewage into it. What with bad sewage and so many seamen from foreign parts, there was a lot of disease and plenty to keep the doctor busy.

My father also gave much of his time to the scattered farms in his practice. But often the most testing times came when tempestuous seas and storms on Doom Bar and in Hell's Bay, as it was called locally, caused shipwrecks, injuries and sometimes deaths when bodies were washed up on the rocks. It is said that the sand came into the estuary about the reign of Henry VIII. I have drawings of the wrecks over the years. I think there were about 300 and a number in the harbour itself. Her father was always at hand in an emergency.

Someone who knew Frank Harvey told me 'The difference between doctor and vicar in country life can be a thin one. He was not only physician but sympathetic counsellor on many family problems. He was often the family's best friend.'

The modern National Health Service has brought increased medical services to the areas to which Dr Harvey gave his youth and his prime. But in his day it was the human spirit that battled against the odds of communication, transport and medical resources.

The more I move around Cornwall, speaking to and recording folk of every kind, the more I sense that throughout the villages, the small coastal and inland towns, against the conspiracies of storm, hard toil and misfortunes there was built up a defensive shield of spontaneous goodwill where ordinary people gave of their best. It was this spirit which has seen the county through its ups and downs in the struggle to survive. It has survived with dignity due to men and women like Frank and Adela Harvey.

ROBERT ROWE

Hospital Attendant

In 1918, when I was nineteen years old, on the battlefield at Cambrai I was walking with a full-size pickaxe slung across my kit-bag, its points resting on top of my pack. The pick pressed heavily on the back of my neck. I came under fire of machine-gun bullets and was wounded.

One bullet passed sideways through my pack, hit the canteen, went through my bread and cheese and passed out on the other side. When I heard the ping of that bullet, I was down on the ground in a flash, otherwise I would have been wounded more seriously. When I went down, the pick hit me on the back of the neck and nearly knocked me out.

When I was demobbed, I got a job as attendant in what was then St Lawrence's Asylum, Bodmin, where I was to devote the next thirty-six years to caring for those who, certified by two doctors and a magistrate, were classed as insane. At that time there were 1,300 patients, about 700 men and 600 women. Today that number is greatly decreased. In those days little research was done into the relationship between the human brain and physical reactions, or on the efficacy of drugs or electrical treatment, and the word madness covered a depth of ignorance. Also, the training of nurses for mental institutions was in its infancy. For three years I studied mental health, sat and passed the necessary exams and qualified as a staff nurse. I became deputy-in-charge, then charge nurse and finished, forty years later, as assistant chief nurse of the hospital.

I had joined the service in 1919 with some apprehension because I knew I had to qualify in three years, which was not easy for someone with an elementary education. I was, however, thankful to have a job at all, having just returned wounded from France, to find over two million unemployed.

Looking back today it all seems primitive, for the methods

137

were those of mechanical restraint, strait-jackets, dungeon, and padded cells, with shower baths each morning as punishment for wetting the bed. Unexpected things were always likely to happen when you were dealing with sadly deranged people. I recall an incident when a completely naked patient clambered through an open window and climbed up a drain-pipe onto the roof of the Kendall building where he remained for three hours. He was as agile as a monkey and the damage he did was considerable. Cars were stationary in the Dunmere for three hours as people watched this incident. The patient stood in the guttering and if this had collapsed he would certainly have crashed to his death. A pair of trousers were placed on the fire-escape ladder for him and it was this that finally induced him to come down. One of the staff managed to grab him by the ankle. Needless to say he was placed in a strait-jacket for some period after that.

I remember when the only way to deal with violent patients, before drugs were discovered, was to put them into strait-jackets. The sleeves came down over the man's hands and the tapes on the end, like sail-cloth, were pulled across the body in front and tied behind so that the man couldn't move. That's all gone now. In my day there were also the padded rooms where the walls were padded with leather so that a man couldn't hurt himself. Even the floors and ceilings were padded. The strait-jackets and padded rooms show how ignorant we were then about the violent mentally handicapped. It was a great step forward when drugs became available.

Before I retired they were trying many new techniques: for example they were operating on the brain, doing pre-frontal leucotomies, in which they separated the frontal lobe from the rear lobe. They experimented with prolonged narcosis, that is putting people to sleep to lessen anxieties and the application of electrodes to administer violent shock. At one time, general paralysis of the insane was practically incurable. It was tragic to watch. When a man died, he looked like a trussed up fowl. His bent legs came up to his chin; his arms were bent too and his eyes would stare upwards at the ceiling, quite helpless.

It was a great day when they learned how to help the paralysis by the introduction of what we called malaria blood, which they injected. I saw it at first up in York where a man was being bitten by a mosquito. That was the initial phase. The malaria germ was stronger than the germs which caused the paralysis; it induced a high temperature of 105°. But it did the trick and I think it was one of the most advanced treatments that came along during the time that I was looking after these patients. There was nothing like it before.

I spent fifteen years of my service on permanent night duty – twenty-eight consecutive nights on duty followed by five off. We did a sixty-hour week and during night duty pegged a clock on the hour and half-hour to show we were alert and not asleep. If you missed too many times you were dismissed for neglect of duty. We had our meals on the ward and the total of our pay was £10 a month. However in those days you had some cheerful episodes. I remember there was a prolonged drought about 1922. The medical superintendent thought it best to sleep the patients of some wards out on the lawn by day and night. I remember asking one old patient one morning how he was getting on. 'Bloody awful,' he replied, 'they left the bloody window open all night!'

There are some patients that should never be released. It is better for them personally and for society that they stay where they can be cared for. I remember a man who the medical superintendent thought should be allowed home to stay with his sister. I had been close to him and I knew, and the staff knew too, that he was very unpredictable. He wasn't a suitable person to go home. One day he was put out in the yard chopping sticks. I suppose his sister must have said something to him and he reacted violently. He had the chopper in his hand and he chopped her down. He was brought to court and judged insane and sent to Broadmoor. Now, I knew Harry and he knew me and I could treat him according to his needs. But he was sent to Broadmoor for twenty-five years. Twenty-five years after his conviction I had retired but I went back one evening to see a friend who worked at St Lawrence's. He told me Harry was back from Broadmoor and asked if I'd like to see him.

I went along and there was Harry with a nurse in charge. He peered at me and said 'I know you, your're Mr Rowe.' He looked much older, as was to be expected after twenty-five years in Broadmoor. I shook him by the hand and told him if he should want for anything to let me know. 'No thank you, Mr

139

Rowe', he said, 'I don't want no money. I've got everything here.' He was a bit breathless but in his day he had been handy with his hands; he could have been a professional boxer. The years in Broadmoor had taken their toll. The sad thing is that he should never have been let out of here in the first place and we, who had been in close contact with him, knew better than anyone what was best for him.

There's the other side of the coin. There were some who I knew were artful and shouldn't have been here in the first place. They enjoyed what in fact was good living. But as time went on and we learned to understand people better, I think most of those who were taking advantage were weeded out. But you've got to get to know people and make friends before you can come to a judgement about them.

A lot of credit for the progress at St Lawrence's in recent years should go to Mrs Banham who became chairman of the Cornwall and Isles of Scilly Area Health Authority. The food and furnishing, the well-being and care of the patients is excellent. Indeed my wife and I have expressed the view that we wouldn't mind spending a month's holiday at St Lawrence's. The old twenty-foot-long bare tables with basins for tea have gone. It is now really a first-class hotel service. In my early days of service every patient was certified. Some arrived handcuffed to a policeman. Everybody had a fear of being taken to Bodmin Asylum, as once admitted, they were seldom visited by relatives as many could not afford to travel from distant parts of the county. Some patients never returned home but died in the hospital, some of them after fifty or sixty years there.

Since the last century the Clifdens have given generously to the development of hospitals in Cornwall, such as Redruth, Bodmin and East Cornwall Hospital whose foundation stone was laid by Lord Clifden. The interest from investments by the Clifdens was allocated to the League of Friends of St Lawrence's, who used it to have an extension built onto the hospital.

When Viscount Clifden became ill and needed constant nursing, he turned to me. Although I had retired from St Lawrence's I was glad to serve him. It was a rewarding experience. Although I constantly emphasised to the Viscount that I was a nurse and not a doctor, he often turned to me for advice. When we were together, there was no side to him. He used to say, 'Where there's sickness, we're all the same.' When his sister fell and broke a femur, I happened to be at the house and was the first to diagnose it. I telephoned her doctor and she was taken to the hospital in Truro. I developed a great respect for the Clifden family.

I had many a good laugh. Once during the night, the Viscount said he was hungry. As the housekeeper had prepared sandwiches for me I said, 'I've got sandwiches. Would you like some?' I brought him the sandwiches which he ate and then he said, 'Where did these sandwiches come from?' I told him his housekeeper had cut them for me. 'Well,' he said, 'they're delicious; she doesn't provide sandwiches like that for me.' The following day, John the butler told me that His Lordship had told him about the sandwiches, adding 'The housekeeper's never made sandwiches like that for me; I hope she isn't in love with him!'

Robert Rowe is a gentle compassionate man, approaching ninety, to whom changing public attitudes towards mental disability, together with scientific knowledge and drug treatments have given great satisfaction. Through a daily realisation of their needs over many years, he gained a deep understanding of his patients as individuals. One of his friends told me 'He was never front page news. He was an ordinary chap doing a difficult job. He's one of God's backroom boys.'

AMY BESWETHERICK

District Nurse

Amy Beswetherick is ninety-one. She is the daughter of a farmer at St Neot, and was the eldest of seven children, some of whom emigrated to America, Australia and Africa.

Amy married a farmer who was severely wounded in the First World War, and was sent to hospital in Cornwall. He died a few years after they were married, leaving her with two daughters aged three and four whom she had to rear with the help of five shillings a week from the Salvation Army. She decided to train to be a district nurse and during this time an understanding granny cared for the two little girls. She now lives quietly and happily in Lostwithiel. The district nurse, who used to ride the Cornish lanes on her tricycle bringing comfort and help to hundreds of Cornish women, tells her own story.

I learned a lot during my training in Plymouth about midwifery and general district nursing. I've still got my examination papers and my certificates from the General Midwives Board. I did my midwifery at Greenbank Hospital. I started as a district nurse in the parish of Grampound and Sticker but after a short time I became district nurse for the parish of Lanlivery and Lanhydrock where I was to spend many happy years. When I was at Grampound I broke my leg and I've still got a silver plate with seven screws to keep the bone together. I got a tricycle, so for many years I was known as the-district-nurse-who-rides-a-tricycle.

Every parish had a district nurse at that time and the system was helped by a subscription. People were asked to pay four shillings and tuppence a year towards the upkeep of the district nurses. Farmers paid more, they paid ten shillings. Mrs Wood, the vicar's wife, was the treasurer for the contributions and Miss Violet Agar-Robartes of Lanhydrock House was the secretary. The subscriptions were voluntary but it was accepted

46 Harry Champion, 2nd World War Light Infantryman
47 Green keeper at St Enodoc Golf CLub
48 John and Mary May with their 9 children

49 The gatehouse at Lanhydrock, where May children went to Sunday school
50 The Hon. Misses Everilda and Violet Robartes attending children at a
   village tea party

51   Esme Dawe, Mayor of Bodmin in a mayorial procession

52   Richard and Esme Dawe,
       mayors of Bodmin

53   Owie Jewell, Honoured Burgess
of Bodmin

54   John Corin, bank manager

55 Mr Corin at the ruins of his ancestor the smuggler John Corlyon's cottage

56 John studying a painting of the Battle of Algiers, 1816, in which Corlyon took part

57 Dr Frank Harvey and his two daughters

58 The Padstow ferry used by passengers to Rock including John Betjeman and Dr Harvey

59   Robert Rowe at St Lawrence's Hospital

60   Amy Beswetherick,
     district nurse

61   Amy at the age of 92

62   Lily May being interviewed by the author with the BBC film unit at her old
     Lanhydrock school, where Elizabeth McGuigan taught

that if you didn't pay you really weren't expected to send for the nurse. Sometimes a person would send for me and they'd say 'Oh, I paid my subscription this morning, Nurse.' My salary was £120 a year and I was paid once a month.

I learned to be very careful about what I said because you were meeting people all the time and they would tell each other that Nurse had said this or that. For instance Miss Robartes would want to know about all her tenants but you had to be discreet. I liked Miss Robartes; she was free and not stuck-up. She'd buy ice-creams for us both when we were in the shop and we'd eat them together. A district nurse had to get on with everybody, the rich and the poor. You belonged to everybody. You were invited to weddings and you saw the wedding dress before the marriage.

There was a report on the district nurse every year, all about her work and the number of visits she made and so on and the secretary and treasurer were at the meeting. You see, when I came home each evening I had to write up all the cases I had attended that day, so at the meeting each year the people who were there heard all about my work.

I was working in a rural area. The farmers were really good. They knew me and if I had to go out to a farm, they'd tell me to make sure I was fetched by a car rather than let me go out at night on my own. If a baby was born, the farmer would give me my dinner on the farm so that I didn't need to go home and come back again. It wasn't just Cornish pasties either. The farmers and their families would have a real cooked meal and you shared it. It was a happy life among the farming folk.

I was the school nurse too, so I'd visit the schools at Lanhydrock and Lanlivery. You had to keep an eye on the pupils for anything that might be wrong with them, a thing like impetigo or other ailments. Children were always having cuts or falling. Then at times you had to visit Lanhydrock House to attend any of the servants if anything was wrong. One day the doctor told me Miss Violet Agar-Robartes, Viscount Clifden's sister, had hurt her hand so I had to go and attend to that. The Robartes gave a dinner each year for their tenants and I was invited.

There was a gypsy camp on the moor near Sweetshouse and they'd come to me too. As I said, the district nurse belonged to everybody. One day one of them came for me to attend his wife. I went out there and did what I had to and told them I was ready to go.

The gypsy said 'Don't ee know the way home?'

'You fetched the district nurse', I said 'and I've come all this way out. Now you've got to see me home. You're responsible.'

So he saw me home. People sometimes ask if I was afraid. Well, in those days you had a job to do and you did it. If a gypsy had a baby, it was your job to see that baby into the world.

I kept in touch with the doctors, and saw them when necessary. When I had to go a long distance, too long for a tricycle, they'd take me and they'd tell me to say how long I'd be and then they would pick me up and take me home. The doctors practised in Lostwithiel.

A number of people in the area had diabetes and the doctors expected me to deal with them. Some would come before going to work each day and I'd give them their insulin injection. I'd go out and see others in their homes. I'd train people to do the injections themselves but I had to test their urine once a week and report to the doctors. I saw the sick people and it was up to me whether to send for the doctor or not.

Sometimes they'd tell me they couldn't afford to pay for the doctor and I'd say, 'But its necessary for you to see the doctor; however I'll come back again this evening and see how you're feeling.'

Many an evening I went back to look after patients because they couldn't afford to pay the doctor. If a person was really poor and had nobody to look after them, it was my responsibility to suggest they go into hospital to be cared for and I had a form to fill in to do this; after that their treatment whether by a doctor or in hospital was free. All my visits around Lanhydrock and Lanlivery were done on my tricycle. I couldn't cycle because I was never brought up to ride a cycle on the farm. I always rode on horseback or with a pony and jingle.

Usually when a mother was going to have a baby, they would tell me, but some wouldn't book me till the eighth month. Of course neighbours in those days were very good and they would look after each other. I liked them to book before they were three months pregnant. But the gypsies who lived on the moor wouldn't be booked and they'd expect me to go out to them at a day's notice. 'Nurse, my Missus is expecting tomorrow,' just like that.

After the baby was born, in those days, the mother would stay in bed for ten days to give her a rest. A woman might have ten children and if she was lucky maybe a sister would come in to help her and after about a week she'd go back to her own house. Of course there were many who weren't so lucky. There were no washing machines, so for a mother it was back to the wash-tub and piles of ironing. It's different today when a mother can come home from hospital after the birth. There's more help around. But it was necessary then for a mother to have a rest. They were kept in bed for their own sake. Before the birth you'd visit her maybe once a week or if you were passing and make out a report for the doctor. You just kept an eye on her and used your own judgement about her getting a doctor free. When the baby was born I'd try to fit in two visits a day for the first three days, then once a day for roughly ten days. If it was a farm worker's wife and the baby arrived in the morning, I'd make a point of seeing it again in the afternoon and it was then the farmers asked me to stay for lunch.

In those days there used to be certain women who would go round and be with the mothers for maybe a fortnight after they had their baby. They were not trained in any way. They would be sent for and paid for by the persons themselves if they could afford it. Some of these women might even stay a month. They would keep the house going till the mother was strong enough to take over.

After I had worked very hard for many years as a district nurse the doctor advised me to take a rest for a while. After that I got the job of night staff nurse in the midwifery section of Redruth Hospital. I got a local bus each day to Lostwithiel and a train from there to Redruth.

I looked after twenty-two mothers and babies in an annexe of the hospital. The people of the hospital welcomed me with open arms. With another nurse I was sent to London for a month on a refresher course.

When I was a girl, we had a pony and jingle on the farm as well as horses. Our canon who was a rich bachelor was the first to have a motor car and he would give Sunday-school children a ride in it. We used to go to parties at each others' houses with the pony and jingle, and on horseback. Often farmers would stay the night and come back in the morning in time for the milking. We all learned to ride and drive. When I got married I got the pony and jingle and I would take butter and eggs, vegetables and that sort of thing into Liskeard to sell to people. When my husband died I had to sell our smallholding and think about the girls' future. So the farmer's daughter and the farmer's wife became the district nurse on her tricycle. I've had two good daughters, and in those early years they worked hard and looked after the house although I've done what I could. I'm proud of them. I have three grandchildren and two great-grandchildren. When I retired for good I was given a lovely tea set. I've been very happy in my work.